The Most Brilliant Thoughts of All Time

(IN TWO LINES OR LESS)

The Most Brilliant Thoughts of All Time

(IN TWO LINES OR LESS)

Edited by John M. Shanahan

Cliff Street Books

An Imprint of HarperCollins*Publishers*

HarperCollins books may be purchased for educational, business, or sales promotional use. For information please write: Special Markets Department, HarperCollins Publishers, Inc., 10 East 53rd Street, New York, NY 10022.

FIRST EDITION

Designed by Phil Mazzone

Library of Congress Cataloging-in-Publication Data
  Most brilliant thoughts of all time : in two lines or less / [edited by]
      John M. Shanahan. — 1st. ed.
          p.   cm.
      ISBN 0-06-019411-1
      1. Quotations, English. 2. Wit and humor. I. Shanahan, John.
  PN6084.HM67   1999
  082—dc21   99-13454

00 01 02 01   ❖   10 9

CONTENTS

"There are two ways of spreading light: to be the candle or the mirror that reflects it."

—*Edith Wharton, 1862–1937*

ACKNOWLEDGMENTS

My thanks to all who helped so much:

Cheryl Skigin
Thomas Arendt
Philip Clarke
Judy Cords
Sue Fenner
Melissa Gibson
Deborah Morris
Thelma Reese
Diane Reverand
Randy Thomas
and
Sean in Dublin

This is the book that will arm you with the most brilliant, delicious thoughts of all time in two lines or less. If you enjoy sharp scalding wit, turn to chapter 1 and read on. However, we must warn you . . . these quotes are highly addictive and may become habit forming. And, above all, after reading this book, you should:

"Never engage in a battle of wits with an unarmed person."

—*Anonymous*,
chapter 6, p. 138

John M. Shanahan

1

The Human Condition

Wit makes its own welcome and levels all distinctions.

Ralph Waldo Emerson, 1803–1882

He who is most creative conceals his sources the best.

Anonymous

We are inclined to believe those whom we do not know because they have never deceived us.

Dr. Samuel Johnson, 1709–1784

The graveyards are full of indispensable men.

Charles de Gaulle, 1890–1970

To think is to say *no*.

Émile Auguste Chartier, 1868–1951

When we ask advice we are usually looking for an accomplice.

Charles Varlet Marquis de La Grange, 1639–1692

If you don't bring Paris with you, you won't find it there.

John M. Shanahan, 1939–

Clever liars give details, but the cleverest don't.

Anonymous

The opposite of talking isn't listening. The opposite of talking is waiting.

Fran Lebowitz, 1950–

Nobody forgets where he buried the hatchet.

Frank McKinney "Kin" Hubbard, 1868–1930

It is a golden rule not to judge men by their opinions but rather by what their opinions make of them.

Georg Christoph Lichtenberg, 1742–1799

Have a care, therefore, where there is more sail than ballast.

William Penn, 1644–1718

Fortune does not change men; it unmasks them.

Suzanne Necker, 1739–1794

The wicked are always surprised to find that the good can be clever.

Luc de Clapiers de Vauvenargues, 1715–1747

It is hard to believe that a man is telling the truth when you know that you would lie if you were in his place.

Henry Louis Mencken, 1880–1956

Rudeness is the weak man's imitation of strength.

Eric Hoffer, 1902–1983

Conscience is the inner voice that warns us somebody may be looking.

Henry Louis Mencken, 1880–1956

Men are not hanged for stealing horses, but that horses may not be stolen.

George Savile, Marquess de Halifax, 1633–1695

Money is like a sixth sense without which you cannot make a complete use of the other five.

William Somerset Maugham, 1874–1965

Remember that in giving any reason at all for refusing, you lay some foundation for a future request.

Sir Arthur Helps, 1813–1875

Most people are other people. Their thoughts are someone else's opinions, their lives a mimicry, their passions a quotation.

Oscar Wilde, 1854–1900

Some circumstantial evidence is very strong, as when you find a trout in the milk.

Henry David Thoreau, 1817–1862

A team effort is a lot of people doing what I say.

Michael Winner, 1935–

Moderation is the last refuge for the unimaginative.

Oscar Wilde, 1854–1900

Reality is the other person's idea of how things should be.

John M. Shanahan, 1939–

Everybody wants to be somebody: Nobody wants to grow.

Johann Wolfgang von Goethe, 1749–1834

One can always be kind to people about whom one cares nothing.

Oscar Wilde, 1854–1900

Better make a weak man your enemy than your friend.

Josh Billings [Henry Wheeler Shaw], 1818–1885

How many pessimists end up by desiring the things they fear, in order to prove that they are right?

Robert Mallett, 1915–

The best you get is an even break.

Franklin P. Adams, 1868–1941

It is no tragedy to do ungrateful people favors, but it is unbearable to be indebted to a scoundrel.

François, Duc de La Rochefoucauld, 1613–1680

To the man who is afraid everything rustles.

Sophocles, c. 496–406 B.C.

In the world a man will often be reputed to be a man of sense, only because he is not a man of talent.

Sir Henry Taylor, 1800–1886

Nothing knits man to man like the frequent passage from hand to hand of cash.

Walter Richard Sickert, 1860–1942

Many know how to please, but know not when they have ceased to give pleasure.

Sir Arthur Helps, 1813–1875

That all men are equal is a proposition to which, at ordinary times, no sane individual has ever given his assent.

Aldous Leonard Huxley, 1894–1963

For many men that stumble at the threshold are well foretold that danger lurks within.

William Shakespeare, 1564–1616

Endurance is frequently a form of indecision.

Princess Elizabeth Bibesco, 1897–1945

How many people become abstract as a way of appearing profound!

Joseph Joubert, 1754–1824

A fanatic is a man who does what he thinks the Lord would do if He knew the facts of the case.

Finley Peter Dunne, 1865–1936

Whoso would be a man must be a nonconformist.

Ralph Waldo Emerson, 1803–1882

One's real life is often the life that one does not lead.

Oscar Wilde, 1854–1900

It is well to remember that the entire population of the universe, with one trifling exception, is composed of others.

Andrew J. Holmes, 1946

We have to serve ourself many years before we gain our own confidence.

Henry S. Haskins, 1878–1957

The keenest sorrow is to recognize ourselves as the sole cause of all our adversities.

Sophocles, c. 496–406 B.C.

This miserable state is borne by the wretched souls of those who lived without disgrace and without praise.

Dante Alighieri, 1265–1321

As I know more of mankind I expect less of them, and am ready now to call a man a good man upon easier terms than I was formerly.

Dr. Samuel Johnson, 1709–1784

Everyone is perfectly willing to learn from unpleasant experience—if only the damage of the first lesson could be repaired.

Georg Christoph Lichtenberg, 1742–1799

A loving person lives in a loving world. A hostile person lives in a hostile world: everyone you meet is your mirror.

Ken Keyes Jr., 1921-1995

The offender never pardons.

George Herbert, 1593–1633

Distrust all those who love you extremely upon a very slight acquaintance and without any visible reason.

Lord Philip Dormer Stanhope Chesterfield, 1694–1773

Women do not find it difficult nowadays to behave like men, but they often find it extremely difficult to behave like gentlemen.

Sir Compton Mackenzie, 1883–1972

No human thing is of serious importance.

Plato, c. 428–348 B.C.

It is the nature of all greatness not to be exact.

Edmund Burke, 1729–1797

Almost all absurdity of conduct arises from the imitation of those whom we cannot resemble.

Dr. Samuel Johnson, 1709–1784

To others we are not ourselves but a performer in their lives cast for a part we do not even know that we are playing.

Princess Elizabeth Bibesco, 1897–1945

Adversity introduces a man to himself.

Anonymous

There are more fools than knaves in the world, else the knaves would not have enough to live upon.

Samuel Butler, 1612–1680

We have no more right to consume happiness without producing it than to consume wealth without producing it.

George Bernard Shaw, 1856–1950

A cathedral, a wave of a storm, a dancer's leap, never turn out to be as high as we had hoped.

Marcel Proust, 1871–1922

When the well's dry, we know the worth of water.

Benjamin Franklin, 1706–1790

I present myself to you in a form suitable to the relationship I wish to achieve with you.

Luigi Pirandello, 1867–1936

Our years, our debts, and our enemies are always more numerous than we imagine.

Charles Nodier, 1780–1844

Experience is not what happens to a man. It is what a man does with what happens to him.

Aldous Leonard Huxley, 1894–1963

You can discover what your enemy fears most by observing the means he uses to frighten you.

Eric Hoffer, 1902–1983

Only dead fish swim with the stream.

Anonymous

He who can lick can bite.

French proverb

All the people like us are We, and everyone else is They.

Rudyard Kipling, 1865–1936

Whatever you condemn, you have done yourself.

Georg Groddeck, 1866–1934

When the fight begins within himself, a man's worth something.

Robert Browning, 1812–1889

When people do not respect us we are sharply offended; yet deep down in his heart no man much respects himself.

Mark Twain [Samuel Langhorne Clemens], 1835–1910

With someone who holds nothing but trumps, it is impossible to play cards.

Christian Freidrich Hebbel, 1813–1863

It's always been and always will be the same in the world: The horse does the work and the coachman is tipped.

Anonymous

Biographies are but the clothes and buttons of the man—the biography of the man himself cannot be written.

Mark Twain [Samuel Langhorne Clemens], 1835–1910

Experience is the name everyone gives to his mistakes.

Oscar Wilde, 1854–1900

One has not the right to betray even a traitor. Traitors must be fought, not betrayed.

Charles Pierre Peguy, 1873–1914

Mediocrity is a hand-rail.

Charles Louis de Secondat, Baron de Montesquieu, 1689–1750

Many are stubborn in pursuit of the path they have chosen, few in pursuit of the goal.

Friedrich Wilhelm Nietzsche, 1844–1900

We seek our happiness outside ourselves, and in the opinion of men we know to be flatterers, insincere, unjust, full of envy, caprice and prejudice.

Jean de La Bruyère, 1645–1695

By a small sample we may judge of the whole piece.

Miguel de Cervantes, 1547–1616

Those who do not feel pain seldom think that it is felt.

Dr. Samuel Johnson, 1709–1784

The dearer a thing is, the cheaper as a general rule we sell it.

Samuel Butler, 1835–1902

Beggars should be abolished. It annoys one to give to them, and it annoys one not to give to them.

Friedrich Wilhelm Nietzsche, 1844–1900

No man does anything from a single motive.

Samuel Taylor Coleridge, 1772–1834

To do great work, a man must be very idle as well as very industrious.

Samuel Butler, 1835–1902

It is easier to resist at the beginning than at the end.

Leonardo da Vinci, 1452–1519

Vows begin when hope dies.

Leonardo da Vinci, 1452–1519

If you can't bite, don't show your teeth.

Yiddish proverb

Nothing so much prevents our being natural as the desire to seem so.

François, Duc de La Rochefoucauld, 1613–1680

To measure up to all that is demanded of him, a man must overestimate his capacities.

Johann Wolfgang von Goethe, 1749–1834

A man who exposes himself when he is intoxicated has not the art of getting drunk.

Dr. Samuel Johnson, 1709–1784

The trouble with using experience as a guide is that the final exam often comes first and then the lesson.

Anonymous

Scoundrels are always sociable.

Arthur Schopenhauer, 1788–1860

He was like a cock who thought the sun had risen to hear him crow.

George Eliot [Marian Evans Cross], 1819–1880

Self-respect is the root of discipline: The sense of dignity grows with the ability to say no to oneself.

Abraham Joshua Heschel, 1907–1972

The greatest mistake you can make in life is to be continually fearing you will make one.

Elbert Hubbard, 1856–1915

You cannot have power for good without having power for evil too. Even mother's milk nourishes murderers as well as heroes.

George Bernard Shaw, 1856–1950

Our names are labels, plainly printed on the bottled essence of our past behavior.

Logan Pearsall Smith, 1865–1946

The way to get things done is not to mind who gets the credit of doing them.

Benjamin Jowett, 1817– 1893

Be not angry that you cannot make others as you wish them to be, since you cannot make yourself as you wish to be.

Thomas à Kempis, 1380–1471

There are many things that we would throw away, if we were not afraid that others might pick them up.

Oscar Wilde, 1854–1900

The chief merit of language is clearness, and we know that nothing detracts so much from this as do unfamiliar terms.

Galen, 129–199

Say not you know another entirely, till you have divided an inheritance with him.

Johann Kasper Lavater, 1741–1801

People hate those who make them feel their own inferiority.

Lord Philip Dormer Stanhope Chesterfield, 1694–1773

Self-love is the greatest of all flatterers.

François, Duc de La Rochefoucauld, 1613–1680

People count up the faults of those who are keeping them waiting.

French proverb

Most men pursue pleasure with such breathless haste that they hurry past it.

Søren Kierkegaard, 1813–1855

All men are tempted. There is no man that lives that can't be broken down, provided it is the right temptation, put in the right spot.

Henry Ward Beecher, 1813–1887

A favor well bestowed is almost as great an honor to him who confers it as to him who receives it.

Sir Richard Steele, 1672–1729

We often make people pay dearly for what we think we give them.

Comtesse Diane [Marie Josephine de Suin de Beausac], 1829–1899

As soon as we attract enough attention in the world to play a part in it, we are set rolling like a ball which will never again be at rest.

Charles Joseph, Prince de Ligne, 1735–1814

A very popular error—having the courage of one's convictions: Rather it is a matter of having the courage for an attack upon one's convictions.

Friedrich Wilhelm Nietzsche, 1844–1900

No one who deserves confidence ever solicits it.

John Churton Collins, 1848–1908

Could we know what men are most apt to remember, we might know what they are most apt to do.

George Savile, Marquess de Halifax, 1633–1695

Never claim as a right what you can ask as a favor.

John Churton Collins, 1848–1908

A man cannot be too careful in the choice of his enemies.

Oscar Wilde, 1854–1900

Our repentance is not so much regret for the ill we have done as fear of the ill that may happen to us in consequence.

François, Duc de La Rochefoucauld, 1613–1680

A hurtful act is the transference to others of the degradation which we bear in ourselves.

Simone Weil, 1909–1943

The gentle mind by gentle deeds is known. For a man by nothing is so well betrayed, as by his manners.

Edmund Spenser, 1552–1599

Man, being responsible, must get drunk; the best of life is but intoxication.

George Noel Gordon, Lord Byron, 1788–1824

It wasn't raining when Noah built the ark.

Howard Ruff, 1930

The greatest pleasure I have known is to do a good action by stealth, and to have it found out by accident.

Charles Lamb, 1775–1834

Chaos often breeds life, when order breeds habit.

Henry Brooks Adams, 1838–1918

When a fellow says it hain't the money but the principle o' the thing, it's th' money.

Frank McKinney "Kin" Hubbard, 1868–1930

There is luxury in self-reproach. When we blame ourselves, we feel no one else has a right to blame us.

Oscar Wilde, 1854–1900

There is no need to show your ability before everyone.

Baltasar Gracian, 1601–1658

There is not, perhaps, to a mind well instructed, a more painful occurrence, than the death of one we have injured without reparation.

Dr. Samuel Johnson, 1709–1784

Many people wait throughout their whole lives for the chance to be good in their own fashion.

Friedrich Wilhelm Nietzsche, 1844–1900

People seem not to see that their opinion of the world is also a confession of character.

Ralph Waldo Emerson, 1803–1882

He gives twice who gives promptly.

Publilius Syrus, first century B.C.

A guest sticks a nail in the wall even if he stays but one night.

Polish proverb

In baiting a mouse trap with cheese, always leave room for the mouse.

Saki [Hector Hugh Monro], 1870–1916

On the heights it is warmer than those in the valley imagine.

Friedrich Wilhelm Nietzsche, 1844–1900

Men show their character in nothing more clearly than by what they think laughable.

Johann Wolfgang von Goethe, 1749–1834

Who well lives, long lives; for this age of ours should not be numbered by years, days, and hours.

Guillaume de Salluste Du Bartas, 1544–1590

One never dives into the water to save a drowning man more eagerly than when there are others present who dare not take the risk.

Friedrich Wilhelm Nietzsche, 1844–1900

Few men have been admired by their own households.

Michel Eyquem de Montaigne, 1533–1592

Violence and injury enclose in their net all that do such things, and generally return upon him who began.

Lucretius [Tirus Lucretius Carus], 99–55 B.C.

There are people who so arrange their lives that they feed themselves only on side dishes.

José Ortega y Gasset, 1883–1955

The path of social advancement is, and must be, strewn with broken friendships.

Herbert George Wells, 1866–1946

Don't shout for help at night, you may wake your neighbors.

Stanislaw Jerzy Lec, 1909–1966

Those who make their dress a principal part of themselves, will, in general, become of no more value than their dress.

William Hazlitt, 1778–1830

A talent is formed in stillness, a character in the world's torrent.

Charles James Fox, 1749–1806

Popularity? It is glory's small change.

Victor Hugo, 1802–1885

Love of fame is the last thing even learned men can bear to be parted from.

Cornelius Tacitus, c. 56–120

Such seems to be the disposition of man, that whatever makes a distinction produces rivalry.

Dr. Samuel Johnson, 1709–1784

To be happy, we must not be too concerned with others.

Albert Camus, 1913–1960

Things sweet the taste prove in digestion sour.

William Shakespeare, 1564–1616

There are no perfectly honorable men; but every true man has one main point of honor and a few minor ones.

George Bernard Shaw, 1856–1950

Sports do not build character. They reveal it.

Heywood Broun, 1888–1939

A man with a career can have no time to waste upon his wife and friends; he has to devote it wholly to his enemies.

John Oliver Hobbes [Pearl Mary Teresa Craigie], 1867–1906

An appeaser is one who feeds a crocodile, hoping that it will eat him last.

Sir Winston Spencer Churchill, 1874–1965

No man is rich enough to buy back his past.

Oscar Wilde, 1854–1900

Pale Death with impartial tread beats at the poor man's cottage door and at the palaces of kings.

Horace [Quintus Horatius Flaccus], 65–8 B.C.

He that hath the name to be an early riser may sleep till noon.

James Howell, c. 1594–1666

Cultivate only the habits that you are willing should master you.

Elbert Hubbard, 1856–1915

To do just the opposite is also a form of imitation.

Georg Christoph Lichtenberg, 1742–1799

There is but an inch of difference between the cushioned chamber and the padded cell.

Gilbert Keith Chesterton, 1874–1936

It is the end that crowns us, not the fight.

Robert Herrick, 1591–1674

A fashion is nothing but an induced epidemic.

George Bernard Shaw, 1856–1950

There are persons who, when they cease to shock us, cease to interest us.

F. H. Bradley, 1846–1924

Nothing is impossible for the man who doesn't have to do it himself.

A. H. Weiler, 1909–1943

Either a good or a bad reputation outruns and gets before people wherever they go.

Lord Philip Dormer Stanhope Chesterfield, 1694–1773

Habits form a second nature.

Jean Baptiste Lamarck, 1744–1829

When people are free to do as they please, they usually imitate each other.

Eric Hoffer, 1902–1983

Don't buy the house; buy the neighborhood.

Russian proverb

Good families are generally worse than any others.

Anthony Hope [Anthony Hope Hawkins], 1863–1933

Life at court does not satisfy a man, but it keeps him from being satisfied with anything else.

Jean de La Bruyère, 1645–1695

The best things and best people rise out of their separateness; I'm against a homogenized society because I want the cream to rise.

Robert Frost, 1874–1963

Without the aid of prejudice and custom, I should not be able to find my way across the room.

William Hazlitt, 1778–1830

If Columbus had an advisory committee he would probably still be at the dock.

Justice Arthur Goldberg, 1908–1990

A hotel isn't like a home, but it's better than being a house guest.

William Feather, 1908–1976

Thousands upon thousands are yearly brought into a state of real poverty by their great anxiety not to be thought poor.

Robert Mallett, 1915–

A committee of one gets things done.

Joe Ryan, 1951–

Those not present are always wrong.

Phillipe Destouches, 1680–1754

Upper classes are a nation's past; the middle class is its future.

Ayn Rand, 1905–1982

Men that cannot entertain themselves want somebody, though they care for nobody.

George Savile, Marquess de Halifax, 1633–1695

Assassination is the extreme form of censorship.

George Bernard Shaw, 1856–1950

Originality is nothing but judicious imitation.

Voltaire [François Marie Arouet], 1694–1778

Unhappiness is best defined as the difference between our talents and our expectations.

Edward de Bono, 1933–

In a tavern everybody puts on airs except the landlord.

Ralph Waldo Emerson, 1803–1882

Blame-all and Praise-all are two blockheads.

Benjamin Franklin, 1706–1790

Injustice is relatively easy to bear; it is justice that hurts.

Henry Louis Mencken, 1880–1956

In the choice of a horse and a wife, a man must please himself, ignoring the opinion and advice of friends.

George John Whyte-Melville, 1821–1878

Like our shadows, our wishes lengthen as our sun declines.

Edward Young, 1683–1765

Riches do not consist in the possession of treasures, but in the use made of them.

Napoleon I, 1769–1821

Opinion is ultimately determined by the feelings, and not by the intellect.

Herbert Spencer, 1820–1903

Humanity is composed but of two categories, the invalids and the nurses.

Richard Brinsley Sheridan, 1751–1816

The future is purchased by the present.

Dr. Samuel Johnson, 1709–1784

What is a committee? A group of the unwilling, picked from the unfit, to do the unnecessary.

Richard Long Harkness, 1907–

When the wine goes in, strange things come out.

Johann Christoph Friedrich von Schiller, 1775–1854

As if you could kill time without injuring eternity.

Henry David Thoreau, 1817–1862

What is originality? Undetected plagiarism.

Dean William Ralph Inge, 1860–1954

All animals are equal, but some animals are more equal than others.

George Orwell [Eric Blair], 1903–1950

The most savage controversies are those about matters as to which there is no good evidence either way.

Bertrand Arthur William Russell, 1872–1970

Next to knowing when to seize an opportunity, the most important thing in life is to know when to forego an advantage.

Benjamin Disraeli, Earl of Beaconsfield, 1804–1881

There are two ways of spreading light: to be the candle or the mirror that reflects it.

Edith Wharton, 1862–1937

I tell you the past is a bucket of ashes.

Carl Sandburg, 1878–1967

We prove what we want to prove, and the real difficulty is to know what we want to prove.

Émile Auguste Chartier, 1868–1951

When everyone is against you, it means that you are absolutely wrong— or absolutely right.

Albert Guinon, 1863–1923

I am more afraid of an army of one hundred sheep led by a lion than an army of one hundred lions led by a sheep.

Charles Maurice, Prince de Talleyrand-Périgord, 1754–1838

To ridicule philosophy is really to philosophize.

Blaise Pascal, 1623–1662

Experience does not err; it is only your judgment that errs in expecting from her what is not in her power.

Leonardo da Vinci, 1452–1519

The greatest grossness sometimes accompanies the greatest refinement, as a natural relief.

William Hazlitt, 1778–1830

In the pursuit of nonconformity, we become the ultimate conformist. Van Gogh was a true nonconformist.

John M. Shanahan, 1939–

In creating, the only hard thing's to begin; a grass-blade's no easier to make than an oak.

James Russell Lowell, 1819–1891

The fire which seems extinguished often slumbers beneath the ashes.

Pierre Corneille, 1606–1684

Living well is the best revenge.

George Herbert, 1593–1633

Anyone who can handle a needle convincingly can make us see a thread which is not there.

E. H. Gombrich, 1909–

The people who are most bigoted are the people who have no convictions at all.

Gilbert Keith Chesterton, 1874–1936

Silence is argument carried on by other means.

Ernesto "Che" Guevara, 1928–1967

To a great experience one thing is essential, an experiencing nature. It is not enough to have opportunity; it is essential to feel it.

Walter Bagehot, 1826–1877

Life is not long, and too much of it must not pass in idle deliberation how it shall be spent.

Dr. Samuel Johnson, 1709–1784

The closing years of life are like the end of a masquerade party, when the masks are dropped.

Arthur Schopenhauer, 1788–1860

Fish die belly-upward and rise to the surface; it is their way of falling.

André Gide, 1869–1951

Social tact is making your company feel at home, even though you wish they were.

Anonymous

It is the property of fools, to be always judging.

Thomas Fuller, 1654–1734

If you take too long in deciding what to do with your life, you'll find you've done it.

George Bernard Shaw, 1856–1950

To deny A is to put A behind bars.

Paul Valéry, 1871–1945

When the mouse laughs at the cat, there's a hole nearby.

Nigerian proverb

The unexamined life is not worth living.

Socrates, 469–399 B.C.

Trust everyone, but cut the cards.

Finley Peter Dunne, 1865–1936

Religion is a man using a divining rod. Philosophy is a man using a pick and shovel.

Anonymous

Doors don't slam open.

John M. Shanahan, 1939–

Only the shallow know themselves.

Oscar Wilde, 1854–1900

Men of ill judgment oft ignore the good that lies within their hands, till they have lost it.

Sophocles, c. 496–406 B.C.

The fruits of philosophy [are the important thing], not the philosophy itself. When we ask the time, we don't want to know how watches are constructed.

Georg Christoph Lichtenberg, 1742–1799

All the arts and sciences have their roots in the struggle against death.

Saint Gregory of Nyssa, c. 335–394

Never mistake motion for action.

Ernest Hemingway, 1899–1961

The enemies of the future are always the very nicest people.

Christopher Morley, 1890–1957

The road up and the road down is one and the same.

Heraclitus, c. 540–c. 480 B.C.

Absence is to love what wind is to fire; it extinguishes the small, it inflames the great.

Roger de Bussy-Rabutin, 1618–1693

There is so much trouble in coming into the world, and so much more, as well as meanness, in going out of it, that 'tis hardly worth while to be here at all.

Viscount Henry St. John Bolingbroke, 1678–1751

The tragedy of life is not so much what men suffer, but rather what they miss.

Thomas Carlyle, 1795–1881

Well begun is half done.

Aristotle, 384–322 B.C.

Everyone is a moon, and has a dark side which he never shows to anybody.

Mark Twain [Samuel Langhorne Clemens], 1835–1910

Be a good animal, true to your animal instincts.

David Herbert Lawrence, 1885–1930

Our civilization is founded on the shambles, and every individual existence goes out in a lonely spasm of helpless agony.

William James, 1842–1910

Wait for that wisest of all counselors, Time.

Pericles, c. 495–429 B.C.

Death twitches my ear. "Live," he says, "I am coming."

Virgil [Publius Vergilius Maro], 70–19 B.C.

A great flame follows a little spark.

Dante Alighieri, 1265–1321

In small proportions we just beauties see, And in short measures life may perfect be.

Ben Jonson, c. 1573–1637

If we would please in society, we must be prepared to be taught many things we know already by people who do not know them.

Sebastien Roch Nicolas Chamfort, 1741–1794

Ill habits gather by unseen degrees—As brooks make rivers, rivers run to seas.

John Dryden, 1631–1700

The test of good manners is to be patient with bad ones.

> *Gabirol [Solomon ben Yehuda ibn Gabirol], c. 1022–c. 1070*

It's but little good you'll do a-watering the last year's crops.

> *George Eliot [Marian Evans Cross], 1819–1880*

One must be something to be able to do something.

> *Johann Wolfgang von Goethe, 1749–1834*

The distance doesn't matter; it is only the first step that is difficult.

> *Marie de Vichy-Chamrond, Marquise du Deffand, 1697–1780*

Women are the simple, and poets the superior artisans of language . . .
the intervention of grammarians is almost always bad.

> *Rémy de Gourmont, 1858–1915*

We often irritate others when we think we could not possibly do so.

> *François, Duc de La Rochefoucauld, 1613–1680*

Perfect behavior is born of complete indifference.

> *Cesare Pavese, 1908–1950*

Use harms and even destroys beauty. The noblest function of an object is to be contemplated.

Miguel de Unamuno, 1864–1936

He knows not his own strength that hath not met adversity.

Ben Jonson, c. 1573–1637

Moral indignation is in most cases 2 percent moral, 48 percent indignation, and 50 percent envy.

Vittorio de Sica, 1901–1974

Dost thou love life? Then do not squander time, for that's the stuff life is made of.

Benjamin Franklin, 1706–1790

Experience is a good teacher, but she sends in terrific bills.

Minna Antrim, 1856–1950

A fanatic is one who can't change his mind and won't change the subject.

Sir Winston Spencer Churchill, 1874–1965

We receive three educations, one from our parents, one from our school-masters, and one from the world. The third contradicts all that the first two teach us.

Charles Louis de Secondat, Baron de Montesquieu, 1689–1750

Worth seeing? Yes, but not worth going to see.

Dr. Samuel Johnson, 1709–1784

A variety of nothing is superior to a monotony of something.

Johann Paul Friedrich Richter, 1763–1825

Won't you come into the garden? I would like my roses to see you.

Richard Brinsley Sheridan, 1751–1816

The average man, who does not know what to do with his life, wants another one which will last forever.

Anatole France [Jacques Anatole François Thibault], 1844–1924

A man's manners are a mirror in which he shows his portrait.

Johann Wolfgang von Goethe, 1749–1834

The love of life is necessary to the vigorous prosecution of any undertaking.

Dr. Samuel Johnson, 1709–1784

Under a tattered cloak you will generally find a good drinker.

Spanish proverb

Simple pleasures . . . are the last refuge of the complex.

Oscar Wilde, 1854–1900

Man is the only animal that can remain on friendly terms with the victims he intends to eat until he eats them.

Samuel Butler, 1835–1902

After three days men grow weary, of a wench, a guest, and weather rainy.

Benjamin Franklin, 1706–1790

People often say that this or that person has not yet found himself. But the self is not something one finds, it is something one creates.

Thomas Szasz, 1920–

Many men are like unto sausages: Whatever you stuff them with, that they will bear in them.

Alexi Konstantinovich Tolstoy, 1817–1875

One does what one is; one becomes what one does.

Robert von Musil, 1880–1942

The gods are those who either have money or do not want it.

Samuel Butler, 1835–1902

Though boys throw stones at frogs in sport, the frogs do not die in sport, but in earnest.

Bion, c. 325–c. 255 B.C.

There are few sorrows, however poignant, in which a good income is of no avail.

Logan Pearsall Smith, 1865–1946

Look for the ridiculous in everything, and you will find it.

Jules Renard, 1864–1910

It is a very delicate job to forgive a man, without lowering him in his estimation, and yours too.

Josh Billings [Henry Wheeler Shaw], 1818–1885

Poverty does not produce unhappiness: It produces degradation.

George Bernard Shaw, 1856–1950

Only mediocrity can be trusted to be always at its best.

Sir Max Beerbohm, 1872–1956

The discovery of a new dish does more for human happiness than the discovery of a new star.

Anthelme Brillat-Savarin, 1755–1826

A diplomatist is a man who always remembers a woman's birthday, but never remembers her age.

Robert Frost, 1874–1963

The people who are regarded as moral luminaries are those who forego ordinary pleasures themselves and find compensation in interfering with the pleasures of others.

Bertrand Arthur William Russell, 1872–1970

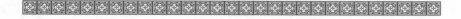

Soup and fish explain half the emotions of life.

Sydney Smith, 1771–1845

Visits always give pleasure—if not the arrival, the departure.

Portuguese proverb

There is no such thing as a pretty good omelet.

French proverb

Waste not fresh tears over old griefs.

Euripides, 485–406 B.C.

A host is like a general: It takes a mishap to reveal his genius.

Horace [Quintus Horatius Flaccus], 65–8 B.C.

Gambling promises the poor what property performs for the rich: That is why the bishops dare not denounce it fundamentally.

George Bernard Shaw, 1856–1950

In the long run, men hit only what they aim at.

Henry David Thoreau, 1817–1862

After a certain age, the more one becomes oneself, the more obvious one's family traits become.

Marcel Proust, 1871–1922

There are people whose watch stops at a certain hour and who remain permanently at that age.

Charles Augustin Sainte-Beuve, 1804–1869

The course of a river is almost always disapproved of by its source.

Jean Cocteau, 1889–1963

A man of fifty is responsible for his face.

Edwin McMasters Stanton, 1814–1869

Old age lives minutes slowly, hours quickly; childhood chews hours and swallows minutes.

Malcolm de Chazal, 1902–1981

There are two things that will be believed of any man whatsoever, and one of them is that he has taken to drink.

Booth Tarkington, 1869–1946

There is no cure for birth and death save to enjoy the interval.

George Santayana, 1863–1952

Once men are caught up in an event they cease to be afraid. Only the unknown frightens men.

Antoine de Saint-Exupéry, 1900–1944

A person is always startled when he hears himself seriously called an old man for the first time.

Oliver W. Holmes Sr., 1806–1894

Egotist, *n.* A person of low taste, more interested in himself than in me.

Ambrose Bierce, 1842–c. 1914

'Tis not the meat, but 'tis the appetite makes eating a delight.

Sir John Suckling, 1609–1642

A man may be so much of everything that he is nothing of anything.

Dr. Samuel Johnson, 1709–1784

The beginning is the most important part of the work.

Plato, c. 428–348 B.C.

Whatever you may be sure of, be sure of this: That you are dreadfully like other people.

James Russell Lowell, 1819–1891

An evil name—a drawback at first—sheds luster on old age.

Logan Pearsall Smith, 1865–1946

To fall into habit is to begin to cease to be.

Miguel de Unamuno, 1864–1936

Our repugnance to death increases in proportion to our consciousness of having lived in vain.

William Hazlitt, 1778–1830

Error is a hardy plant: It flourisheth in every soil.

Martin Farquhar Tupper, 1810–1889

Two and two the mathematician continues to make four, in spite of the whine of the amateur for three, or the cry of the critic for five.

James McNeill Whistler, 1834–1903

All that Adam had, all that Caesar could, you have and can do. . . . Build, therefore, your own world.

Ralph Waldo Emerson, 1803–1882

We grow weary of those things (and perhaps soonest) which we most desire.

Samuel Butler, 1612–1680

We do not do what we want and yet we are responsible for what we are— that is the fact.

Jean Paul Sartre, 1905–1980

Youth is a blunder; manhood a struggle; old age a regret.

Benjamin Disraeli, Earl of Beaconsfield, 1804–1881

Everyone is born a king, and most people die in exile.

Oscar Wilde, 1854–1900

Drink not the third glass, which thou canst not tame when once it is within thee.

George Herbert, 1593–1633

If disorder is the rule with you, you will be penalized for installing order.

Paul Valéry, 1871–1945

The minority is always right.

Henrik Johan Ibsen, 1828–1906

Men are made by nature unequal. It is vain, therefore, to treat them as if they were equal.

James Anthony Froude, 1818–1894

Resolve to be thyself; and know that he who finds himself, loses his misery.

Matthew Arnold, 1822–1888

You can never plan the future by the past.

Edmund Burke, 1729–1797

Possessions are usually diminished by possession.

Friedrich Wilhelm Nietzsche, 1844–1900

Civilization: a thin veneer over barbarianism.

John M. Shanahan, 1939–

Great blunders are often made, like large ropes, of a multitude of fibers.

Victor Hugo, 1802–1885

To really enjoy the better things in life, one must first have experienced the things they are better than.

Oscar Holmolka, 1898–1978

I cling to my imperfection, as the very essence of my being.

Anatole France [Jacques Anatole François Thibault], 1844–1924

If you pick up a starving dog and make him prosperous, he will not bite you. This is the principal difference between a dog and a man.

Mark Twain [Samuel Langhorne Clemens], 1835–1910

It is easier to cope with a bad conscience than with a bad reputation.

Friedrich Wilhelm Nietzsche, 1844–1900

Most people return small favors, acknowledge medium ones, and repay great ones—with ingratitude.

Benjamin Franklin, 1706–1790

There is in a man an upwelling spring of life, energy, love, whatever you like to call it. If a course is not cut for it, it turns the ground round it into a swamp.

Mark Rutherford [William Hale White], 1831–1913

The mill cannot grind with the water that's past.

George Herbert, 1593–1633

Man is the only animal who causes pain to others with no other object than wanting to do so.

Arthur Schopenhauer, 1788–1860

A fool always finds a greater fool to admire him.

Nicholas Boileau-Despreaux, 1636–1711

Leave off wishing to deserve any thanks from anyone, thinking that anyone can ever become grateful.

Galius Valerius Catullus, 87–c. 54 B.C.

If I try to be like him, who will be like me?

Yiddish proverb

Almost everything that is great has been done by youth.

Benjamin Disraeli, Earl of Beaconsfield, 1804–1881

Individualism is rather like innocence: There must be something unconscious about it.

Louis Kronenberger, 1904–1980

I now perceive one immense omission in my psychology—the deepest principle of Human Nature is the craving to be appreciated.

William James, 1842–1910

Life is like playing a violin solo in public and learning the instrument as one goes along.

Samuel Butler, 1835–1902

I like men who have a future and women who have a past.

Oscar Wilde, 1854–1900

Once conform, once do what others do because they do it, and a kind of lethargy steals over all the finer senses of the soul.

Michel Eyquem de Montaigne, 1533–1592

When we feel that we lack whatever is needed to secure someone else's esteem, we are very close to hating him.

Luc de Clapiers de Vauvenargues, 1715–1747

We always like those who admire us; we do not always like those whom we admire.

François, Duc de La Rochefoucauld, 1613–1680

He who is outside his door already has the hard part of his journey behind him.

Dutch proverb

Some people are so fond of ill luck that they run halfway to meet it.

Douglas William Jerrold, 1803–1857

We judge ourselves by what we feel capable of doing, while others judge us by what we have already done.

Henry Wadsworth Longfellow, 1807–1882

Many a crown shines spotless now that yet was deeply sullied in the winning.

Johann Christoph Friedrich von Schiller, 1775–1854

In a calm sea every man is a pilot.

John Ray, 1627–1705

Jesters do oft prove prophets.

William Shakespeare, 1564–1616

An unfulfilled vocation drains the color from a man's entire existence.

Honoré de Balzac, 1799–1850

The friendship that can cease has never been real.

Saint Jerome, c. 342–420

The most decisive actions of our life . . . are most often unconsidered actions.

André Gide, 1869–1951

The gratitude of most men is merely a secret desire to receive greater benefits.

François, Duc de La Rochefoucauld, 1613–1680

Things are always at their best in the beginning.

Blaise Pascal, 1623–1662

Love your neighbor, yet pull not down your hedge.

George Herbert, 1593–1633

All the trouble in the world is due to the fact that man cannot sit still in a room.

Blaise Pascal, 1623–1662

The first blow is half the battle.

Oliver Goldsmith, 1728–1774

Since we are mortal, friendships are best kept to a moderate level, rather than sharing the very depths of our souls.

Euripides, 485–406 B.C.

You may be disappointed if you fail, but you are doomed if you don't try.

Beverly Sills, 1929–

To show resentment at a reproach is to acknowledge that one may have deserved it.

Cornelius Tacitus, c. 56–120

Those who have given themselves the most concern about the happiness of peoples have made their neighbors very miserable.

Anatole France [Jacques Anatole François Thibault], 1844–1924

There is no kind of idleness by which we are so easily seduced as that which dignifies itself by the appearance of business.

Dr. Samuel Johnson, 1709–1784

Whoever has his foe at his mercy, and does not kill him, is his own enemy.

Sa'di [Musharrif-uddin], 1184–1291

In prosperity our friends know us; in adversity we know our friends.

John Churton Collins, 1848–1908

Treat your friend as if he might become an enemy.

Publilius Syrus, first century B.C.

We will either find a way, or make one.

Hannibal, 247–183 B.C.

Early impressions are hard to eradicate from the mind. When once wool has been dyed purple, who can restore it to its previous whiteness?

Saint Jerome, c. 342–420

Evil deeds do not prosper; the slow man catches up with the swift.

Homer, c. 700 B.C.

Trust only movement. Life happens at the level of events, not of words. Trust movement.

Alfred Adler, 1870–1937

No guest is so welcome in a friend's house that he will not become a nuisance after three days.

Titus Maccius Plautus, 254–184 B.C.

We have three kinds of friends: those who love us, those who are indifferent to us, and those who hate us.

Sebastien Roch Nicolas Chamfort, 1741–1794

The buyer needs a hundred eyes, the seller not one.

George Herbert, 1593–1633

He makes no friend who never made a foe.

Alfred Lord Tennyson, 1809–1892

The haft of the arrow had been feathered with one of the eagle's own plumes. We often give our enemies the means of our own destruction.

Aesop, c. 550 B.C.

Friend is sometimes a word devoid of meaning; enemy, never.

Victor Hugo, 1802–1885

He who has a thousand friends has not a friend to spare, and he who has one enemy will meet him everywhere.

Ali ibn-Abi-Talib, c. 602–661

Beware of entrance to a quarrel, but, being in, bear 't that th' opposed may beware of thee.

William Shakespeare, 1564–1616

No one can make you feel inferior without your consent.

Anna Eleanor Roosevelt, 1884–1962

Observe due measure, for right timing is in all things the most important factor.

Hesiod, c. 700 B.C.

There are people whom one should like very well to drop, but would not wish to be dropped by.

Dr. Samuel Johnson, 1709–1784

An object in possession seldom retains the same charm that it had in pursuit.

Pliny the Younger [Gaius Plinius Caecilius Secundis], c. 61–c. 112 B.C.

The applause of a single human being is of great consequence.

Dr. Samuel Johnson, 1709–1784

You saw his weakness, and he will never forgive you.

Johann Christoph Friedrich von Schiller, 1775–1854

It is a good rule in life never to apologize. The right sort of people do not want apologies, and the wrong sort take a mean advantage of them.

Sir Pelham Grenville Wodehouse, 1881–1975

Few men make themselves masters of the things they write or speak.

John Selden, 1564–1654

The multitude is always in the wrong.

Dillon Wentworth, Earl of Rosscommon, c. 1633–1685

Anyone can hold the helm when the sea is calm.

Publilius Syrus, first century B.C.

May you have a lawsuit in which you know you are in the right.

Gypsy curse

2

Success, Fortune, Failure, and Misfortune

Fortune does not change men; it unmasks them.

Suzanne Necker, 1739–1794

All men that are ruined, are ruined on the side of their natural propensities.

Edmund Burke, 1729–1797

Success has made failures of many men.

Cindy Adams

It is not enough to succeed. Others must fail.

Gore Vidal, 1925-

Chance does nothing that has not been prepared beforehand.

Alexis de Tocqueville, 1805–1859

Great success is commoner than great abilities.

Luc de Clapiers de Vauvenargues, 1715–1747

If you want to know what a man is really like, take notice how he acts when he loses money.

New England proverb

If a man look sharply and attentively, he shall see fortune; for though she be blind, yet she is not invisible.

Sir Francis Bacon, 1561–1626

Sleep, riches, and health to be truly enjoyed must be interrupted.

Johann Paul Friedrich Richter, 1763–1825

The common excuse of those who bring misfortune on others is that they desire their good.

Luc de Clapiers de Vauvenargues, 1715–1747

Whenever a friend succeeds, a little something in me dies.

Gore Vidal, 1925–

One must be a god to be able to tell successes from failures without making a mistake.

Anton Pavlovich Chekhov, 1860–1904

Failure changes for the better, success for the worse.

Lucius Annaeus Seneca, c. 4 B.C.–65 A.D.

The greatest reverses of fortune are the most easily borne from a sort of dignity belonging to them.

William Hazlitt, 1778–1830

As always, victory finds a hundred fathers, but defeat is an orphan.

Count Galeazzo Ciano, 1903–1944

One likes people much better when they're battered down by a prodigious siege of misfortune than when they triumph.

Virginia Woolf, 1882–1941

He was a self-made man who owed his lack of success to nobody.

Joseph Heller, 1923–

Rich man down and poor man up—they are still not even.

Yiddish proverb

People don't ever seem to realize that doing what's right is no guarantee against misfortune.

William McFee, 1881–1966

It is not impossibilities which fill us with the deepest despair, but possibilities which we have failed to realize.

Robert Mallett, 1915–

We need greater virtues to sustain good fortune than bad.

François, Duc de La Rochefoucauld, 1613–1680

It is often the failure who is the pioneer in new lands, new undertakings, and new forms of expression.

Eric Hoffer, 1902–1983

Some rise by sin, and some by virtue fall.

William Shakespeare, 1564–1616

Whatso'er we perpetrate,/ We do but row; we are steered by fate.

Samuel Butler, 1612–1680

The secret of success in life is known only to those who have not succeeded.

John Churton Collins, 1848–1908

The slave has but one master; the ambitious man has as many as can help in making his fortune.

Jean de La Bruyère, 1645–1695

Fame is the beginning of the fall of greatness.

V. V. Rozanov, 1856–1919

I cannot give you the formula for success, but I can give you the formula for failure, which is—try to please everybody.

Herbert Bayard Swope, 1882–1958

Success is going from failure to failure without a loss of enthusiasm.

Anonymous

Success is not so much what you are, but rather what you appear to be.

Anonymous

Never contend with a man who has nothing to lose.

Baltasar Gracian, 1601–1658

A minute's success pays the failure of years.

Robert Browning, 1812–1889

We never know, believe me, when we have succeeded best.

Miguel de Unamuno, 1864–1936

Nothing fails like success because we don't learn from it. We learn only from failure.

Kenneth Ewart Boulding, 1910–1993

One of the misfortunes of our time is that in getting rid of false shame, we have killed off so much real shame as well.

Louis Kronenberger, 1904–1980

Every man has a right to be conceited until he is successful.

Benjamin Disraeli, Earl of Beaconsfield, 1804–1881

You always pass failure on your way to success.

Mickey Rooney, 1920–

A man's character is his fate.

Heraclitus, c. 540–c. 480 B.C.

The final test of fame is to have a crazy person imagine he is you.

Anonymous

Fame is something like unto a kind of mushroom, which Pliny recounts to be the greatest miracle in nature, because growing and having no root.

Thomas Fuller, 1608–1661

Success is an accident . . . well placed.

John M. Shanahan, 1939–

If you live long enough, you'll see that every victory turns into a defeat.

Simone de Beauvoir, 1908–1986

Calamities are of two kinds. Misfortune to ourselves and good fortune to others.

Ambrose Bierce, 1842–c. 1914

The shortest and best way to make your fortune is to let people see clearly that it is in their interests to promote yours.

Jean de La Bruyère, 1645–1695

All men's misfortunes spring from their hatred of being alone.

Jean de La Bruyère, 1645–1695

In the fields of observation chance favors only the prepared mind.

Louis Pasteur, 1822–1895

Candor and generosity, unless tempered by due moderation, lead to ruin.

Cornelius Tacitus, c. 56–120

It is through chance that, from among the various individuals of which each of us is composed, one emerges rather than another.

Henry de Montherlant, 1896–1972

We all have strength enough to endure the misfortunes of others.

François, Duc de La Rochefoucauld, 1613–1680

You don't hold your own in the world by standing on guard, but by attacking and getting well hammered yourself.

George Bernard Shaw, 1856–1950

Men despise great projects when they do not feel themselves capable of great successes.

Luc de Clapiers de Vauvenargues, 1715–1747

It is better to be adventurous than cautious, because fortune is a woman.

Niccolò Machiavelli, 1469–1527

Cease to ask what the morrow will bring forth, and set down as gain each day that Fortune grants.

Horace [Quintus Horatius Flaccus], 65–8 B.C.

Failure is not the only punishment for laziness; there is also the success of others.

Jules Renard, 1864–1910

Nothing great was ever achieved without enthusiasm.

Ralph Waldo Emerson, 1803–1882

Footprints on the sands of time are not made by sitting down.

Anonymous

You never find people laboring to convince you that you may live very happily upon a plentiful fortune.

Dr. Samuel Johnson, 1709–1784

The value of money is that with it we can tell any man to go to the devil. It is the sixth sense which enables you to enjoy the other five.

William Somerset Maugham, 1874–1965

Fame is proof that the people are gullible.

Ralph Waldo Emerson, 1803–1882

We are dismayed when we find that even disaster cannot cure us of our faults.

Luc de Clapiers de Vauvenargues, 1715–1747

All glory comes from daring to begin.

Anonymous

The deed is everything, the glory nothing.

Johann Wolfgang von Goethe, 1749–1834

Those that have done nothing in life, are not qualified to judge of those that have done little.

Dr. Samuel Johnson, 1709–1784

The first undertakers in all great attempts commonly miscarry, and leave the advantages of their losses to those that come after them.

Samuel Butler, 1612–1680

Striving to better, oft we mar what's well.

William Shakespeare, 1564–1616

Success: The one unpardonable sin against one's fellows.

Ambrose Bierce, 1842–c. 1914

Fortune brings in some boats that are not steer'd.

William Shakespeare, 1564–1616

3

Truth, Lies, and Deception

We are inclined to believe those whom we do not know because they have never deceived us.

Dr. Samuel Johnson, 1709–1784

Clever liars give details, but the cleverest don't.

Anonymous

Nobody forgets where he buried the hatchet.

Frank McKinney "Kin" Hubbard, 1868–1930

It is hard to believe that a man is telling the truth when you know that you would lie if you were in his place.

Henry Louis Mencken, 1880–1956

The height of cleverness is to be able to conceal it.

François, Duc de La Rochefoucauld, 1613–1680

Success has always been a great liar.

Friedrich Wilhelm Nietzsche, 1844–1900

We discover in ourselves what others hide from us, and we recognize in others what we hide from ourselves.

Luc de Clapiers de Vauvenargues, 1715–1747

If we suspect that a man is lying, we should pretend to believe him; for then he becomes bold and assured, lies more vigorously, and is unmasked.

Arthur Schopenhauer, 1788–1860

Our enemies' opinion of us comes closer to the truth than our own.

François, Duc de La Rochefoucauld, 1613–1680

No man of honor ever quite lives up to his code, any more than a moral man manages to avoid sin.

Henry Louis Mencken, 1880–1956

We are much harder on people who betray us in small ways than on people who betray others in great ones.

François, Duc de La Rochefoucauld, 1613–1680

Show me a liar, and I'll show thee a thief.

George Herbert, 1593–1633

We confess to little faults only to persuade ourselves that we have no great ones.

François, Duc de La Rochefoucauld, 1613–1680

He who says there is no such thing as an honest man, you may be sure is himself a knave.

George Bishop Berkeley, 1685–1753

It is impossible for a man to be cheated by anyone but himself.

Ralph Waldo Emerson, 1803–1882

Truth is the safest lie.

Yiddish proverb

Truth is the cry of all, but the game of few.

George Bishop Berkeley, 1685–1753

Man is ice to truth and fire to falsehood.

Jean de La Fontaine, 1621–1695

Nothing is truer in a sense than a funeral oration: It tells precisely what the dead man should have been.

Gustave Vapereau, 1909–1942

That Man, who flees from truth, should have invented the mirror is the greatest of historical miracles.

Christian Freidrich Hebbel, 1813–1863

In great affairs men show themselves as they wish to be seen; in small things they show themselves as they are.

Sebastien Roch Nicolas Chamfort, 1741–1794

Nothing is more damaging to a new truth than an old error.

Johann Wolfgang von Goethe, 1749–1834

All charming people have something to conceal, usually their total dependence on the appreciation of others.

Cyril Connolly, 1903–1974

If you want to keep something concealed from your enemy, do not disclose it to your friend.

Gabirol [Solomon ben Yehuda ibn Gabirol], c. 1022–c. 1070

Truth is a torch that gleams through the fog without dispelling it.

Claude Adrien Helvétius, 1715–1771

We find it easy to believe that praise is sincere: Why should anyone lie in telling us the truth?

Jean Rostand, 1894–1977

Crafty men deal in generalizations.

Anonymous

There are times when lying is the most sacred of duties.

Eugène Marin Labiche, 1815–1888

A man's most valuable trait is a judicious sense of what not to believe.

Euripides, 485–406 B.C.

Many a truth is spoke in jest.

Anonymous

A lie is an abomination unto the Lord and a very present help in trouble.

Adlai Stevenson, 1900–1965

A man has made great progress in cunning when he does not seem too clever to others.

Jean de La Bruyère, 1645–1695

He who does not need to lie is proud of not being a liar.

Friedrich Wilhelm Nietzsche, 1844–1900

Praise and criticism are both frauds.

Anonymous

What is said when drunk has been thought out beforehand.

Flemish proverb

Who lies for you will lie against you.

Bosnian proverb

The cruelest lies are often told in silence.

Adlai Stevenson, 1900–1965

'Tis my opinion every man cheats in his way, and he is only honest who is not discovered.

Susannah Centlivre, c. 1667–1723

Almost all our faults are more pardonable than the methods we resort to hide them.

François, Duc de La Rochefoucauld, 1613–1680

It requires as much caution to tell the truth as to conceal it.

Baltasar Gracian, 1601–1658

Every truth passes through three stages before it is recognized. In the first, it is ridiculed, in the second it is opposed, in the third it is regarded as self-evident.

Arthur Schopenhauer, 1788–1860

In quarreling, the truth is always lost.

Publilius Syrus, first century B.C.

Things are entirely what they appear to be and *behind them* . . . there is nothing.

Jean Paul Sartre, 1905–1980

Convictions are more dangerous foes of truth than lies.

Friedrich Wilhelm Nietzsche, 1844–1900

What probably distorts everything in life is that one is convinced that one is speaking the truth because one says what one thinks.

Sacha Guitry, 1885–1959

When you have eliminated the impossible, whatever remains, however improbable, must be the truth.

Arthur Conan Doyle, 1859–1930

Belief in truth begins with doubting all that has hitherto been believed to be true.

Friedrich Wilhelm Nietzsche, 1844–1900

Appearances are not held to be a clue to the truth. But we seem to have no other.

Dame Ivy Compton-Burnett, 1884–1969

A truth that's told with bad intent beats all the lies you can invent.

William Blake, 1757–1827

One may sometimes tell a lie, but the grimace with which one accompanies it tells the truth.

Friedrich Wilhelm Nietzsche, 1844–1900

If you shut your door to all errors, truth will be shut out.

Rabindranath Tagore, 1861–1941

Some of the most frantic lies on the face of life are told with modesty and restraint; for the simple reason that only modesty and restraint will save them.

Gilbert Keith Chesterton, 1874–1936

Contradiction is not a sign of falsity, nor the lack of contradiction a sign of truth.

Blaise Pascal, 1623–1662

Those who never retract their opinions love themselves more than they love the truth.

Joseph Joubert, 1754–1824

Remember: One lie does not cost you one truth but the truth.

Christian Freidrich Hebbel, 1813–1863

If you speak the truth, have a foot in the stirrup.

Turkish proverb

Give me a fruitful error any time, full of seeds, bursting with its own corrections. You can keep your sterile truth for yourself.

Vilfredo Pareto, 1848–1923

There are only two ways of telling the complete truth—anonymously and posthumously.

Thomas Sowell, 1930–

It is to be believed because it is absurd.

Quintus Septimus Tertullianus, c. 160–c. 240 B.C.

Much truth is spoken, that more may be concealed.

Justice Sir Charles Darling, 1849–1893

The visionary lies to himself, the liar only to others.

Friedrich Wilhelm Nietzsche, 1844–1900

Truth does not blush.

Quintus Septimus Tertullianus, c. 160–c. 240 B.C.

That which has always been accepted by everyone, everywhere, is almost certain to be false.

Paul Valéry, 1871–1945

Everything that deceives may be said to enchant.

Plato, c. 428–348 B.C.

What upsets me is not that you lied to me, but that from now on I can no longer believe you.

Friedrich Wilhelm Nietzsche, 1844–1900

Weak people cannot be sincere.

François, Duc de La Rochefoucauld, 1613–1680

It is a matter of perfect indifference where a thing originated; the only question is: Is it true in and for itself?

Georg Wilhelm Friedrich Hegel, 1770–1831

Men hate those to whom they have to lie.

Victor Hugo, 1802–1885

A smile is the chosen vehicle for all ambiguities.

Herman Melville, 1819–1891

The true way to be deceived is to think oneself more clever than others.

François, Duc de La Rochefoucauld, 1613–1680

He who fondles you more than usual has either deceived you or wants to do so.

French proverb

In human relations kindness and lies are worth a thousand truths.

Graham Greene, 1904–1991

Man, as he is, is not a genuine article. He is an imitation of something, and a very bad imitation.

Peter Demianovich Ouspensky, 1878–1947

All men are born truthful, and die liars.

Luc de Clapiers de Vauvenargues, 1715–1747

Nothing is easier than self-deceit. For what each man wishes, that he also believes to be true.

Demosthenes, c. 384–322 B.C.

It is one thing to show a man that he is in an error, and another to put him in possession of the truth.

John Locke, 1632–1704

Oh, what a tangled web we weave, When first we practice to deceive!

Sir Walter Scott, 1771–1832

The truth is forced upon us, very quickly, by a foe.

Aristophanes, c. 450–385 B.C.

A proof tells us where to concentrate our doubts.

Anonymous

Suspect him the most who trusts the least.

Anonymous

Though it be honest, it is never good to bring bad news.
William Shakespeare, 1564–1616

The most certain way to hide from others the limits of our knowledge is not to go beyond them.

Count Giacomo Leopardi, 1798–1837

To be sincere means to be the same person when one is with oneself; that is to say, alone—but that is all it means.

Paul Valéry, 1871–1945

One's own self is well hidden from one's own self; of all mines of treasure, one's own is the last to be dug up.

Friedrich Wilhelm Nietzsche, 1844–1900

There is great skill in knowing how to conceal one's skill.

François, Duc de La Rochefoucauld, 1613–1680

When you are unwilling to sacrifice or conceal any of your abilities their reputation is generally diminished.

Luc de Clapiers de Vauvenargues, 1715–1747

Unlike grownups, children have little need to deceive themselves.

Johann Wolfgang von Goethe, 1749–1834

4

Talk, Talk, Talk

When we ask advice we are usually looking for an accomplice.

Charles Varlet de La Grange, 1639–1692

The opposite of talking isn't listening. The opposite of talking is waiting.

Fran Lebowitz, 1950–

Remember that in giving any reason at all for refusing, you lay some foundation for a future request.

Sir Arthur Helps, 1813–1875

Criticism is prejudice made plausible.

Henry Louis Mencken, 1880–1956

We rarely confide in those who are better than we are.

Albert Camus, 1913–1960

So long as men praise you, you can only be sure that you are not yet on your own true path but on someone else's.

Friedrich Wilhelm Nietzsche, 1844–1900

No one gossips about other people's secret virtues.

Bertrand Arthur William Russell, 1872–1970

Trust not him with your secrets, who, when left alone in your room, turns over your papers.

Johann Kasper Lavater, 1741–1801

He who praises everybody, praises nobody.

James Boswell, 1740–1795

We bestow on others praise in which we do not believe, on condition that in return they bestow upon us praise in which we do.

Jean Rostand, 1894–1977

The vow that binds too strictly snaps itself.

Alfred Lord Tennyson, 1809–1892

If you would convince others, seem open to conviction yourself.

Lord Philip Dormer Stanhope Chesterfield, 1694–1773

None but a coward dares to boast that he has never known fear.

Ferdinand Marshall Foch, 1851–1929

We are generally the better persuaded by the reasons we discover ourselves than by those given to us by others.

Blaise Pascal, 1623–1662

You can take better care of your secret than another can.

Ralph Waldo Emerson, 1803–1882

Usually we praise only to be praised.

François, Duc de La Rochefoucauld, 1613–1680

We are more anxious to speak than to be heard.

Henry David Thoreau, 1817–1862

In science, the credit goes to the man who convinces the world, not to the man to whom the idea first occurs.

Sir William Osler, 1849–1919

A secret may be sometimes best kept by keeping the secret of its being a secret.

Sir Henry Taylor, 1800–1886

Explaining is generally half confessing.

George Savile, Marquess de Halifax, 1633–1725

Nobody will keep the thing he hears to himself, and nobody will repeat just what he hears and no more.

Lucius Annaeus Seneca, c. 4 B.C.–65 A.D.

None are more taken in by flattery than the proud, who wish to be the first and are not.

Benedict Spinoza, 1632–1677

When a man say him do not mind, then him mind.

Southern proverb

When you have nothing to say, say nothing.

Charles Caleb Colton, 1780–1832

He who praises you for what you lack wishes to take from you what you have.

Don Juan Manuel, 1282–1349

We only confess our little faults to persuade people that we have no large ones.

François, Duc de La Rochefoucauld, 1613–1680

Never speak ill of yourself, your friends will always say enough on that subject.

Charles Maurice, Prince de Talleyrand-Périgord, 1754–1838

Conscience is thoroughly well bred and soon leaves off talking to those who do not wish to hear it.

Samuel Butler, 1835–1902

The louder he talked on his honor, the faster we counted our spoons.

Ralph Waldo Emerson, 1803–1882

Lovers never get tired of each other, because they are always talking about themselves.

François, Duc de La Rochefoucauld, 1613–1680

They always talk who never think.

Matthew Prior, 1664–1721

Who are next to knaves? Those that converse with them.

Alexander Pope, 1688–1744

When a proud man hears another praised, he feels himself injured.

English proverb

To refuse praise reveals a desire to be praised twice over.

François, Duc de La Rochefoucauld, 1613–1680

Never tell your resolution beforehand.

John Selden, 1584–1654

Nothing is more despicable than a professional talker who uses his words as a quack uses his remedies.

François de Salignac de la Mothe Fénelon, 1651–1715

No one means all he says, and yet very few say all they mean, for words are slippery and thought is viscous.

Henry Brooks Adams, 1838–1918

The best way to find out if a man has done something is to advise him to do it. He will not be able to resist boasting that he has done it without being advised.

Comtesse Diane [Marie Josephine de Suin de Beausacq], 1829–1899

The best way to keep one's word is not to give it.

Napoleon I, 1769–1821

Blessed is the man who, having nothing to say, abstains from giving in words evidence of the fact.

George Eliot [Marian Evans Cross], 1819–1880

It is the dread of something happening, something unknown and dreadful, that makes us do anything to keep the flicker of talk from dying out.

Logan Pearsall Smith, 1865–1946

There is no such thing as conversation. It is an illusion. There are intersecting monologues, that is all.

Dame Rebecca West [Cicily Maxwell Andrews], 1892–1983

Two may talk and one may hear, but three cannot take part in a conversation of the most sincere and searching sort.

Ralph Waldo Emerson, 1803–1882

Beware of the conversationalist who adds "in other words." He is merely starting afresh.

Christopher Morley, 1890–1957

A bore is a man who deprives you of solitude without providing you with company.

Gian Vincenzo Gravina, 1664–1718

Nothing seems to me so inane as bookish language in conversation.

Marie-Henri Beyle Stendhal [Henri Beyle], 1783–1843

He who is slowest in making a promise is most faithful in its performance.

Jean Jacques Rousseau, 1712–1778

An injury is much sooner forgotten than an insult.

Lord Philip Dormer Stanhope Chesterfield, 1694–1773

Never trust a man who speaks well of everybody.

John Churton Collins, 1848–1908

Bore, *n.* A person who talks when you wish him to listen.

Ambrose Bierce, 1842–c. 1914

There is no refuge from confession but suicide; and suicide is confession.

Daniel Webster, 1782–1852

Those that merely talk and never think, that live in the wild anarchy of drink.

Ben Jonson, c. 1573–1637

He is not praised whose praiser deserveth not praise.

Gabriel Harvey, 1545–1630

No man is exempt from saying silly things; the mischief is to say them deliberately.

Michel Eyquem de Montaigne, 1533–1592

Talkers are no good doers.

William Shakespeare, 1564–1616

The secret of being a bore is to tell everything.

Voltaire [François Marie Arouet], 1694–1778

So long as there is any subject which men may not freely discuss, they are timid upon all subjects.

John Jay Chapman, 1862–1933

If I have said something to hurt a man once, I shall not get the better of this by saying many things to please him.

Dr. Samuel Johnson, 1709–1784

A little inaccuracy sometimes saves tons of explanation.

Saki [Hector Hugh Monro], 1870–1916

A powerful idea communicates some of its power to the man who contradicts it.

Marcel Proust, 1871–1922

Speech is the small change of silence.

George Meredith, 1828–1909

Sometimes we deny being worthy of praise, hoping to generate an argument we would be pleased to lose.

Cullen Hightower

Be advised that all flatterers live at the expense of those who listen to them.

Jean de La Fontaine, 1621–1695

Silence propagates itself, and the longer talk has been suspended, the more difficult it is to find anything to say.

Dr. Samuel Johnson, 1709–1784

Tell me to what you pay attention and I will tell you who you are.

José Ortega y Gasset, 1883–1955

To do all the talking and not be willing to listen is a form of greed.

Democritus of Abdera, c. 460–c. 370 B.C.

We often refuse to accept an idea merely because the tone of voice in which it has been expressed is unsympathetic to us.

Friedrich Wilhelm Nietzsche, 1844–1900

Three may keep a secret, if two of them are dead.

Benjamin Franklin, 1706–1790

Silence is the most perfect expression of scorn.

George Bernard Shaw, 1856–1950

Never believe anything until it has been officially denied.

Claud Cockburn, 1904–1981

Who cannot give good counsel? 'Tis cheap; it costs them nothing.

Robert Burton, 1577–1640

You lose it if you talk about it.

Ernest Hemingway, 1899–1961

A fool hath no dialogue within himself; the first thought carrieth him without the reply of a second.

George Savile, Marquess de Halifax, 1633–1695

A fair request should be followed by the deed in silence.

Dante Alighieri, 1265–1321

A wise man hears one word and understands two.

Jewish proverb

He who cannot love must learn to flatter.

Johann Wolfgang von Goethe, 1749–1834

To give a reason for anything is to breed a doubt of it.

William Hazlitt, 1778–1830

We always weaken whatever we exaggerate.

Jean François de La Harpe, 1739–1803

Every individual or national degeneration is immediately revealed by a directly proportional degradation in language.

Joseph-Marie de Maistre, 1753–1821

There are people who, instead of listening to what is being said to them, are already listening to what they are going to say themselves.

Albert Guinon, 1863–1923

Words, like eyeglasses, blur everything that they do not make more clear.

Joseph Joubert, 1754–1824

The habit of common and continuous speech is a symptom of mental deficiency. It proceeds from not knowing what is going on in other people's minds.

Walter Bagehot, 1826–1877

Most men make little use of their speech than to give evidence against their own understanding.

George Savile, Marquess de Halifax, 1633–1695

The time to stop talking is when the other person nods his head affirmatively but says nothing.

Henry S. Haskins, 1878–1957

Words signify man's refusal to accept the world as it is.

Walter Kaufmann, 1921–1980

Tact is after all a kind of mind-reading.

Sarah Orne Jewett, 1849–1909

Listen or thy tongue will keep thee deaf.

American Indian proverb

How can I tell what I think till I see what I say?

Edward Morgan Forster, 1879–1970

Look wise, say nothing, and grunt. Speech was given to conceal thought.

Sir William Osler, 1849–1919

She understood how much louder a cock can crow in its own farmyard than elsewhere.

Anthony Trollope, 1815–1882

One often makes a remark and only later sees how true it is.

Ludwig Wittgenstein, 1889–1951

Every man becomes, to a certain degree, what the people he generally converses with are.

Lord Philip Dormer Stanhope Chesterfield, 1694–1773

It is almost impossible to state what one in fact believes, because it is almost impossible to hold a belief and to define it at the same time.

Charles Williams, 1886–1945

A timid question will always receive a confident answer.

Justice Sir Charles Darling, 1849–1893

A definition is the enclosing a wilderness of idea within a wall of words.

Samuel Butler, 1835–1902

Never praise a sister to a sister, in the hope of your compliments reaching the proper ears.

Rudyard Kipling, 1865–1936

Before using a fine word, make a place for it!

Joseph Joubert, 1754–1824

One says a lot in vain, refusing; The other mainly hears the "No."

Johann Wolfgang von Goethe, 1749–1834

There are some occasions when a man must tell half his secret, in order to conceal the rest.

Lord Philip Dormer Stanhope Chesterfield, 1694–1773

It is always a silly thing to give advice, but to give good advice is fatal.

Oscar Wilde, 1854–1900

Men use thought only to justify their wrongdoings, and speech only to conceal their thoughts.

Voltaire [François Marie Arouet], 1694–1778

Sometimes we think we dislike flattery, but it is only the way it is done that we dislike.

François, Duc de La Rochefoucauld, 1613–1680

Oaths are but words, and words but wind.

Samuel Butler, 1612–1680

Don't let young people confide in you their aspirations; when they drop them they will drop you.

Logan Pearsall Smith, 1865–1946

Those whose conduct gives room for talk are always the first to attack their neighbors.

Jean Baptiste Poqurlin Molière, 1622–1673

Since Penelope Noakes of Duppas Hill is gone, there is no one who will ever call me Nellie again.

an old lady

We recognize that flattery is poison, but its perfume intoxicates us.

Charles Vartlet, Marquis de la Grange, 1639–1692

Whoever gossips to you will gossip of you.

Spanish proverb

One should never trust a woman who tells one her real age. A woman who would tell one that, would tell one anything.

Oscar Wilde, 1854–1900

He that flatters you more than you desire either has deceived you or wishes to deceive.

Italian proverb

You can tell the character of every man when you see how he receives praise.

Lucius Annaeus Seneca, c. 4 B.C.–65 A.D.

And all who told it added something new, and all who heard it made enlargements too.

Alexander Pope, 1688–1744

The flatterer does not think highly enough of himself or of others.

Jean de La Bruyère, 1645–1695

Generally those who boast most of contentment have least of it. Their very boasting shows that they want something, and barely beg it, namely, commendation.

Thomas Fuller, 1608–1661

We resent all criticism which denies us anything that lies in our line of advance.

Ralph Waldo Emerson, 1803–1882

Ridicule often checks what is absurd, and fully as often smothers that which is noble.

Sir Walter Scott, 1771–1832

The value of an ideal has nothing whatever to do with the sincerity of the man who expresses it.

Oscar Wilde, 1854–1900

Against criticism a man can neither protest nor defend himself; he must act in spite of it, and then it will gradually yield to him.

Johann Wolfgang von Goethe, 1749–1834

He who knows how to flatter also knows how to slander.

Napoleon I, 1769–1821

If a friend is in trouble, don't annoy him by asking if there is anything you can do. Think up something appropriate and do it.

Edgar Watson Howe, 1853–1937

It takes your enemy and your friend, working together, to hurt you to the heart; the one to slander you and the other to get the news to you.

Mark Twain [Samuel Langhorne Clemens], 1835–1910

A flatterer is a man that tells you your opinion and not his own.

Anonymous

Praise undeserved is satire in disguise.

Broadhurst, early eighteenth century

When a man speaks of his strength, he whispers his weakness.

John M. Shanahan, 1939–

You must not pay a person a compliment, and then straightway follow it with a criticism.

Mark Twain [Samuel Langhorne Clemens], 1835–1910

A man seldom gives praise gratis. He commends a qualification in another, but then he would be thought himself to be a master of that qualification.

Anonymous

He only may chastise who loves.

Rabindranath Tagore, 1861–1941

Tact consists in knowing how far to go in going too far.

Jean Cocteau, 1889–1963

He who excuses himself accuses himself.

Gabriel Meurier, 1530–1601

Violence is, essentially, a confession of ultimate inarticulateness.

Time *magazine*

He who praises everybody praises nobody.

Dr. Samuel Johnson, 1709–1784

Nothing is easier than to keep a secret: There needs no more but to shut one's mouth.

Anonymous

5

Passions, Virtues, and Vices

Men's passions are so many roads by which they can be reached.

Luc de Clapiers de Vauvenargues, 1715–1747

Everything that emancipates the spirit without giving us control over ourselves is harmful.

Johann Wolfgang von Goethe, 1749–1834

Rudeness is the weak man's imitation of strength.

Eric Hoffer, 1902–1983

In jealousy there is more self-love than love.

François, Duc de La Rochefoucauld, 1613–1680

Those who are believed to be most abject and humble are usually most ambitious and envious.

Benedict Spinoza, 1632–1677

We are not satisfied to be right, unless we can prove others to be quite wrong.

William Hazlitt, 1778–1830

Women keep a special corner of their hearts for sins they have never committed.

Cornelia Otis Skinner, 1901–1979

As cowardly as a coward is, it is not safe to call a coward a coward.

Anonymous

A man has generally the good or ill qualities which he attributes to mankind.

William Shenstone, 1714–1763

Weak people never give way when they ought to.

Jean François-Paul de Gandi, Cardinal de Retz, 1614–1679

From fanaticism to barbarism is only one step.

Denis Diderot, 1713–1784

Consistency requires you to be as ignorant today as you were a year ago.

Bernard Berenson, 1865–1959

Just as those who practice the same profession recognize each other instinctively, so do those who practice the same vice.

Marcel Proust, 1871–1922

It is well that there is no one without a fault, for he would not have a friend in the world: He would seem to belong to a different species.

William Hazlitt, 1778–1830

When men grow virtuous in their old age, they only make a sacrifice to God of the devil's leavings.

Alexander Pope, 1688–1744

There is not a passion so strongly rooted in the human heart as envy.

Richard Brinsley Sheridan, 1751–1816

A show of envy is an insult to oneself.

Yevgeny Alexandrovich Yevtushenko, 1933–

Consistency is the last refuge of the unimaginative.

Oscar Wilde, 1854–1900

In the human heart new passions are forever being born; the overthrow of one almost always means the rise of another.

François, Duc de La Rochefoucauld, 1613–1680

The weak can never forgive. Forgiveness is the attribute of the strong.

Mohandas Karamchand [Mahatma] Gandhi, 1869–1948

Our greatest pretenses are built up not to hide the evil and the ugly in us, but our emptiness. The hardest thing to hide is something that is not there.

Eric Hoffer, 1902–1983

When you have found out the prevailing passion of any man, remember never to trust him where that passion is concerned.

Lord Philip Dormer Stanhope Chesterfield, 1694–1773

It is difficult to overcome one's passions, and impossible to satisfy them.

Marguerite de La Sablière, late seventeenth century

If we had no faults of our own, we would not take so much pleasure in noticing those of others.

François, Duc de La Rochefoucauld, 1613–1680

Some have been thought brave because they were afraid to run away.

Thomas Fuller, 1654–1734

'Tis not the drinking that is to be blamed, but the excess.

John Selden, 1584–1654

Fanaticism consists in redoubling your effort when you have forgotten your aim.

George Santayana, 1863–1952

Solemnity is a device of the body to hide the faults of the mind.

François, Duc de La Rochefoucauld, 1613–1680

Men's evil manners live in brass; their virtues we write in water.

William Shakespeare, 1564–1616

Almost every man wastes part of his life in attempts to display qualities which he does not possess, and to gain applause which he cannot keep.

Dr. Samuel Johnson, 1709–1784

All passions exaggerate: It is only because they exaggerate that they are passions.

Sebastien Roch Nicolas Chamfort, 1741–1794

An emotion ceases to be a passion as soon as we form a clear and distinct idea of it.

Benedict Spinoza, 1632–1677

Though pride is not a virtue, it is the parent of many virtues.

John Churton Collins, 1848–1908

Humility is a virtue all preach, none practice; and yet everybody is content to hear.

John Selden, 1584–1654

A pious man is one who would be an atheist if the king were.

Jean de La Bruyère, 1645–1695

That which we call sin in others is experiment for us.

Ralph Waldo Emerson, 1803–1882

Pride is generally censured and decried, but mainly by those who have nothing to be proud of.

Arthur Schopenhauer, 1788–1860

Modesty and unselfishness—these are virtues which men praise—and pass by.

André Maurois, 1885–1967

Few love to hear the sins they love to act.

William Shakespeare, 1564–1616

To act from pure benevolence is not possible for finite beings. Human benevolence is mingled with vanity, interest, or some other motive.

Dr. Samuel Johnson, 1709–1784

The follies which a man regrets most are those which he didn't commit when he had the opportunity.

Helen Rowland, 1875–1950

Envy honors the dead in order to insult the living.

Claude Adrien Helvetius, 1715–1771

Patience has its limits. Take it too far, and it's cowardice.

George Jackson, 1941–1971

The vices we scoff at in others, we laugh at within ourselves.

Sir Thomas Browne, 1605–1682

Many would be cowards if they had courage enough.

Thomas Fuller, 1654–1734

Perfect courage means doing unwitnessed what we would be capable of with the world looking on.

François, Duc de La Rochefoucauld, 1613–1680

One of envy's favorite stratagems is the attempt to provoke envy in the envied one.

Leslie Farber, 1912–1981

Envy slays itself by its own arrows.

Anonymous

I prefer an accommodating vice to an obstinate virtue.

Jean Baptiste Poquelin Molière, 1622–1673

We often pride ourselves on even the most criminal passions, but envy is a timid and shamefaced passion we never dare to acknowledge.

François, Duc de La Rochefoucauld, 1613–1680

It has been my experience that folks who have no vices have very few virtues.

Abraham Lincoln, 1809–1865

Virtue is praised but hated. People run away from it, for it is ice-cold, and in this world you must keep your feet warm.

Denis Diderot, 1713–1784

Our virtues and vices couple with one another, and get children that resemble both their parents.

George Savile, Marquess de Halifax, 1633–1695

Beware the fury of a patient man.

John Dryden, 1631–1700

There is no man so good that if he placed all his actions and thoughts under the scrutiny of the laws, he would not deserve hanging ten times in his life.

Michel Eyquem de Montaigne, 1533–1592

Integrity is praised and starves.

Juvenal [Decimus Junius Juvenalis], c. 55–c. 130 A.D.

I have not been afraid of excess: Excess on occasion is exhilarating. It prevents moderation from acquiring the deadening effect of a habit.

William Somerset Maugham, 1874–1965

Artificial manners vanish the moment the natural passions are touched.

Maria Edgeworth, 1767–1849

For neither man nor angel can discern hypocrisy, the only evil that walks invisible.

John Milton, 1608–1674

If we escape punishment for our vices, why should we complain if we are not rewarded for our virtues?

John Churton Collins, 1848–1908

Virtues, like essences, lose their fragrance when exposed.

William Shenstone, 1714–1763

To know your ruling passion, examine your castles in the air.

Archbishop Richard Whately, 1787–1863

Modesty is the only bait when you angle for praise.

Lord Philip Dormer Stanhope Chesterfield, 1694–1773

If it was necessary to tolerate in other people everything that one permits oneself, life would be unbearable.

Georges Courteline, 1860–1929

It is always the secure who are humble.

Gilbert Keith Chesterton, 1874–1936

Procrastination is the thief of time.

Edward Young, 1683–1765

The man who is master of his passions is Reason's slave.

Cyril Connolly, 1903–1974

In our ideals we unwittingly reveal our vices.

Jean Rostand, 1894–1977

I have seen gross intolerance shown in support of tolerance.

Samuel Taylor Coleridge, 1772–1834

Courage is the art of being the only one who knows you're scared to death.

Harold Wilson, Baron of Rievaulx, 1916–1995

Intolerance is natural and logical, for in every dissenting opinion lies an assumption of superior wisdom.

Ambrose Bierce, 1842–c. 1914

Absence diminishes mediocre passions and increases great ones, as the wind blows out candles and fans fire.

François, Duc de La Rochefoucauld, 1613–1680

Rarely do great beauty and great virtue dwell together.

Petrarch [Francesco Petrarca], 1304–1374

It is with our passions as it is with fire and water; they are good servants, but bad masters.

Sir Roger L'Estrange, 1616–1704

You must not think me necessarily foolish because I am facetious, nor will I consider you necessarily wise because you are grave.

Sydney Smith, 1771–1845

At times, our strengths propel us so far forward we can no longer endure our weaknesses and perish from them.

Friedrich Wilhelm Nietzsche, 1844–1900

What the world needs is more geniuses with humility, there are so few of us left.

Oscar Levant, 1906–1972

The belief in a supernatural source of evil is not necessary; men alone are quite capable of every wickedness.

Joseph Conrad, 1857–1924

To be honest, as this world goes, is to be one man picked out of ten thousand.

William Shakespeare, 1564–1616

Jealousy is the fear or apprehension of superiority; envy our uneasiness under it.

William Shenstone, 1714–1763

Idleness is only the refuge of weak minds.

Lord Philip Dormer Stanhope Chesterfield, 1694–1773

People who have no weaknesses are terrible; there is no way of taking advantage of them.

Anatole France [Jacques Anatole François Thibault], 1844–1924

Jealousy feeds upon suspicion, and turns into fury or it ends as soon as we pass from suspicion to certainty.

François, Duc de La Rochefoucauld, 1613–1680

Women's virtue is man's greatest invention.

Cornelia Otis Skinner, 1901–1979

Our culture peculiarly honors the act of blaming, which it takes as the sign of virtue and intellect.

Lionel Trilling, 1905–1976

The jealous are the readiest of all to forgive, and all women know it.

Fedor Dostoevsky, 1821–1881

Jealousy is always born with love, but does not always die with it.

François, Duc de La Rochefoucauld, 1613–1680

To many people virtue consists chiefly in repenting faults, not in avoiding them.

Georg Christoph Lichtenberg, 1742–1799

When the vices give us up we flatter ourselves that we are giving up them.

François, Duc de La Rochefoucauld, 1613–1680

Courage is rightly esteemed the first of human qualities because it is the quality which guarantees all others.

Sir Winston Spencer Churchill, 1874–1965

Nothing sharpens sight like envy.

Thomas Fuller, 1654–1734

The strength of a man's virtue should not be measured by his special
exertions, but by his habitual acts.

Blaise Pascal, 1623–1662

6

It's Only in Your Mind

To think is to say *no*.

Émile Auguste Chartier, 1868–1951

Vision is the art of seeing things invisible.

Jonathan Swift, 1667–1745

Most of one's life . . . is one prolonged effort to prevent oneself thinking.

Aldous Leonard Huxley, 1894–1963

Conscience is the inner voice that warns us somebody may be looking.

Henry Louis Mencken, 1880–1956

Great ideas have a very short shelf life.

John M. Shanahan, 1939–

I often marvel how it is that though each man loves himself beyond all else, he should yet value his own opinion of himself less than that of others.

Marcus Aurelius, 121–180

Reality is the other person's idea of how things should be.

John M. Shanahan, 1939–

Behind many acts that are thought ridiculous there lie wise and weighty motives.

François, Duc de La Rochefoucauld, 1613–1680

A wise man will make more opportunities than he finds.

Sir Francis Bacon, 1561–1626

Conscience warns us before it reproaches us.

Comtesse Diane [Marie Josephine de Suin de Beausacq], 1829–1899

Who reflects too much will accomplish little.

Johann Christoph Friedrich von Schiller, 1775–1854

Every man takes the limits of his own field of vision for the limits of the world.

Arthur Schopenhauer, 1788–1860

People are governed by the head; a kind heart is of little value in chess.

Sebastien Roch Nicolas Chamfort, 1741–1794

Could we know what men are most apt to remember, we might know what they are most apt to do.

George Savile, Marquess de Halifax, 1633–1695

A wise man knows everything; a shrewd one, everybody.

Anonymous

What others think of us would be of little moment did it not, when known, so deeply tinge what we think of ourselves.

Lucius Annaeus Seneca, c. 4 B.C.*–65* A.D.

When a man reaches a condition in which he believes a thing must happen because he does not wish it, and what he wishes to happen can never be, this is called desperation.

Arthur Schopenhauer, 1788–1860

Knowledge can be communicated but not wisdom.

Herman Hesse, 1877–1962

Man is a reasonable animal who always loses his temper when he is called upon to act in accordance with the dictates of reason.

Oscar Wilde, 1854–1900

Good judgment comes from experience, and experience comes from bad judgment.

Barry LePatner

With most men, unbelief in one thing springs from blind belief in another.

Georg Christoph Lichtenberg, 1742–1799

Never engage in a battle of wits with an unarmed person.

Anonymous

Common sense is the collection of prejudices acquired by age eighteen.

Albert Einstein, 1879–1955

Who are a little wise, the best fools be.

John Donne, 1572–1631

Nothing has an uglier look to us than reason, when it is not on our side.

George Savile, Marquess de Halifax, 1633–1695

Conscience is, in most men, an anticipation of the opinion of others.

Sir Henry Taylor, 1800–1886

The woman who thinks she is intelligent demands equal rights with men. A woman who is intelligent does not.

Sidonie-Gabrielle Colette, 1873–1954

No one knows what he is doing so long as he is acting rightly; but of what is wrong one is always conscious.

Johann Wolfgang von Goethe, 1749–1834

Keep off your thoughts from things that are past and done; for thinking of the past wakes regret and pain.

Arthur Waley, 1889–1966

A wise man will keep his suspicions muzzled, but he will keep them awake.

George Savile, Marquess de Halifax, 1633–1695

Mediocre minds usually dismiss anything which reaches beyond their own understanding.

François, Duc de La Rochefoucauld, 1613–1680

Idealism is what precedes experience; cynicism is what follows.

David T. Wolf, 1943–

A wise man sees as much as he ought, not as much as he can.

Michel Eyquem de Montaigne, 1533–1592

A man who is "of sound mind" is one who keeps the inner madman under lock and key.

Paul Valéry, 1871–1945

If someone tells you he is going to make "a realistic decision," you immediately understand that he has resolved to do something bad.

Mary Therese McCarthy, 1912–1989

All our final resolutions are made in a state of mind which is not going to last.

Marcel Proust, 1871–1922

No mind is thoroughly well organized that is deficient in a sense of humor.

Samuel Taylor Coleridge, 1772–1834

To endeavor to forget anyone is a certain way of thinking of nothing else.

Jean de La Bruyère, 1645–1695

I am not young enough to know everything.

Oscar Wilde, 1854–1900

Up to a certain point every man is what he thinks he is.

F. H. Bradley, 1846–1924

The reasons which any man offers to you for his own conduct betray his opinion of your character.

Sir Arthur Helps, 1813–1875

The more intelligent a man is, the more originality he discovers in men. Ordinary people see no difference between men.

Blaise Pascal, 1623–1662

Men of genius are rarely much annoyed by the company of vulgar people.

Samuel Taylor Coleridge, 1772–1834

Almost all rich veins of original and striking speculation have been opened by systematic half-thinkers.

John Stuart Mill, 1806–1873

A man is not necessarily intelligent because he has plenty of ideas, any more than he is a good general because he has plenty of soldiers.

Sebastien Roch Nicolas Chamfort, 1741–1794

There are people who think that everything one does with a serious face is sensible.

Georg Christoph Lichtenberg, 1742–1799

A wise man will live as much within his wit as his income.

Lord Philip Dormer Stanhope Chesterfield, 1694–1773

There is a kinship, a kind of freemasonry, between all persons of intelligence, however antagonistic their moral outlook.

Norman Douglas, 1868–1952

Chi Wen Tzu always thought three times before taking action. Twice would have been quite enough.

Confucius, 551–479 B.C.

Our most important thoughts are those which contradict our emotions.

Paul Valéry, 1871–1945

Dogma does not mean the absence of thought, but the end of thought.

Gilbert Keith Chesterton, 1874–1936

Everybody calls "clear" those ideas which have the same degree of confusion as his own.

Marcel Proust, 1871–1922

There is a great difference between still believing something and believing it again.

Georg Christoph Lichtenberg, 1742–1799

Madness is to think of too many things in succession too fast, or of one thing too exclusively.

Voltaire [François Marie Arouet], 1694–1778

Every great idea exerts, on first appearing, a tyrannical influence: Hence, the advantages it brings are turned all too soon into disadvantages.

Johann Wolfgang von Goethe, 1749–1834

Serious things cannot be understood without laughable things, nor opposites at all without opposites.

Plato, c. 428–348 B.C.

Men who borrow their opinions can never repay their debts.

George Savile, Marquess de Halifax, 1633–1695

It is a profitable thing, if one is wise, to seem foolish.

Aeschylus, 525– 456 B.C.

What was hard to endure is sweet to recall.

Continental proverb

Between cultivated minds the first interview is the best.

Ralph Waldo Emerson, 1803–1882

Opinions have vested interests just as men have.

Samuel Butler, 1835–1902

Nothing that is worth knowing can be taught.

Oscar Wilde, 1854–1900

It were not best that we should all think alike; it is difference of opinion that makes horse-races.

Mark Twain [Samuel Langhorne Clemens], 1835–1910

We are less hurt by the contempt of fools than by the lukewarm approval of men of intelligence.

Luc de Clapiers de Vauvenargues, 1715–1747

Discovery consists of seeing what everybody has seen and thinking what nobody has thought.

Albert von Szent-Gyorgyi, 1893–1986

A man's mind is hidden in his writings; criticism brings it to light.

Gabirol [Solomon ben Yehuda ibn Gabirol], c. 1022–c. 1070

The man who sees both sides of a question is a man who sees absolutely nothing at all.

Oscar Wilde, 1854–1900

The mind of a bigot is like the pupil of the eye; the more light you pour upon it, the more it will contract.

Oliver W. Holmes Jr., 1841–1935

The man who insists upon seeing with perfect clearness before he decides, never decides.

Henri-Frederic Amiel, 1821–1881

The intelligent man finds almost everything ridiculous, the sensible man hardly anything.

Johann Wolfgang von Goethe, 1749–1834

Seeking to know is only too often learning to doubt.

Antoinette du Ligier de la Garde Deshoulières, 1638–1694

Only when we know little do we know anything; doubt grows with knowledge.

Johann Wolfgang von Goethe, 1749–1834

Every great advance in natural knowledge has involved the absolute rejection of authority.

Thomas Henry Huxley, 1825–1895

Stupid sons don't ruin a family; it is the clever ones who do.

Mr. Tut-Tut

Most ignorance is vincible ignorance. We don't know because we don't want to know.

Aldous Leonard Huxley, 1894–1963

It's bad taste to be wise all the time, like being at a perpetual funeral.

David Herbert Lawrence, 1885–1930

The art of being wise is the art of knowing what to overlook.

William James, 1842–1910

A wise man's questions contain half the answer.

Gabirol [Solomon ben Yehuda ibn Gabirol], c. 1022–c. 1070

The mind's direction is more important than its progress.

Joseph Joubert, 1754–1824

Every extreme attitude is a fight from the self.

Eric Hoffer, 1902–1983

Our minds are lazier than our bodies.

François, Duc de La Rochefoucauld, 1613–1680

Having precise ideas often leads to a man doing nothing.

Paul Valéry, 1871–1945

Logic and consistency are luxuries for the gods and the lower animals.

Samuel Butler, 1835–1902

Man is what he believes.

Anton Pavlovich Chekhov, 1860–1904

Be careful how you interpret the world: It is like that.

Erich Heller, 1911–1990

Brains are an asset, if you hide them.

Mae West, 1892–1980

To have doubted one's own first principles is the mark of a civilized man.

Oliver W. Holmes Jr., 1841–1935

Thou hast commanded that an ill-regulated mind should be its own punishment.

Saint Augustine, 354–430

The man who listens to reason is lost: Reason enslaves all whose minds are not strong enough to master her.

George Bernard Shaw, 1856–1950

Nothing is more dangerous than an idea, when it's the only one we have.

Émile Auguste Chartier, 1868–1951

Very simple ideas lie within the reach only of complex minds.

Remy de Gourmont, 1858–1915

Big ideas are so hard to recognize, so fragile, so easy to kill. Don't forget that, all of you who don't have them.

John Elliott Jr., 1937–

Colleges hate geniuses, just as convents hate saints.

Ralph Waldo Emerson, 1803–1882

The things we know best are things we haven't been taught.

Luc de Clapiers de Vauvenargues, 1715–1747

Insanity is often the logic of an accurate mind overtasked.

Oliver W. Holmes Sr., 1806–1894

All intelligent thoughts have already been thought; what is necessary is only to try to think them again.

Johann Wolfgang von Goethe, 1749–1834

To want to forget something is to think of it.

French proverb

A pessimist is a man who thinks all women are bad. An optimist is a man who hopes they are.

Chauncey Mitchell Depew, 1834–1928

A very great memory often forgetteth how much time is lost by repeating things of no use.

George Savile, Marquess de Halifax, 1633–1695

Some people do not become thinkers simply because their memories are too good.

Friedrich Wilhelm Nietzsche, 1844–1900

It is not enough to possess wit. One must have enough of it to avoid having too much.

André Maurois, 1885–1967

Amusement is the happiness of those that cannot think.

Alexander Pope, 1688–1744

Genius is an infinite capacity for taking pains.

Jane Ellis Hopkins, 1836–1904

There are two sides to every question: my side and the wrong side.

Oscar Levant, 1906–1972

Mediocrity knows nothing higher than itself, but talent instantly recognizes genius.

Arthur Conan Doyle, 1859–1930

Why should a man's mind have been thrown into such close, sad, sensational, inexplicable relations with such a precarious object as his body?

Thomas Hardy, 1840–1928

It is well, when one is judging a friend, to remember that he is judging you with the same godlike and superior impartiality.

Arnold Bennett, 1867–1931

Cynicism—the intellectual cripple's substitute for intelligence.

Joseph Russell Lynes Jr., 1910–

The educated man tries to repress the inferior one in himself, without realizing that by this he forces the latter to become revolutionary.

Carl Gustav Jung, 1875–1961

Clear your mind of can't.

Dr. Samuel Johnson, 1709–1784

Style is the dress of thoughts.

Lord Philip Dormer Stanhope Chesterfield, 1694–1773

Genius will live and thrive without training, but it does not the less reward the watering pot and pruning knife.

Margaret Fuller, 1810–1850

Man is equally incapable of seeing the nothingness from which he emerges and the infinity in which he is engulfed.

Blaise Pascal, 1623–1662

Were it not for imagination, sir, a man would be as happy in the arms of a chambermaid as of a duchess.

Dr. Samuel Johnson, 1709–1784

An invasion of armies can be resisted, but not an idea whose time has come.

Victor Hugo, 1802–1885

The more scholastically educated a man is generally, the more he is an emotional boor.

David Herbert Lawrence, 1885–1930

Soon after a hard decision, something inevitably occurs to cast doubt. Holding steady against that doubt usually proves the decision.

R. I. Fitzhenry, 1918–

Whether learning has made more proud men or good men, may be a question.

Anonymous

Who lives without folly is not so wise as he thinks.

François, Duc de La Rochefoucauld, 1613–1680

The stacking together of the paintings of the great masters in museums is a catastrophe, and a collection of a hundred good intellects produces collectively one idiot.

Carl Gustav Jung, 1875–1961

There is no such thing as a great talent without great will-power.

Honoré de Balzac, 1799–1850

Intellect is invisible to the man who has none.

Arthur Schopenhauer, 1788–1860

No man is the wiser for his learning; it may administer matter to work in, or objects to work upon, but wit and wisdom are born with a man.

John Selden, 1584–1654

We never do anything well till we cease to think about the manner of doing it.

William Hazlitt, 1778–1830

Knowledge may give weight, but accomplishments give luster, and many more people see than weigh.

Lord Philip Dormer Stanhope Chesterfield, 1694–1773

Nothing will ever be attempted, if all possible objections must be first overcome.

Dr. Samuel Johnson, 1709–1784

Take time to deliberate; but when the time for action arrives, stop thinking and go in.

Andrew Jackson, 1767–1845

No one is more liable to make mistakes than the man who acts only on reflection.

Luc de Clapiers de Vauvenargues, 1715–1747

We're drowning in information and starving for knowledge.

Rutherford D. Rogers, 1915–

The fool doth think he is wise, but the wise man knows himself to be a fool.

William Shakespeare, 1564–1616

All professional men are handicapped by not being allowed to ignore things which are useless.

Johann Wolfgang von Goethe, 1749–1834

We should rather examine, who is better learned, than who is more learned.

Michel Eyquem de Montaigne, 1533–1592

To be ignorant of one's ignorance is the malady of the ignorant.

Bronson Alcott, 1799–1888

A great deal of learning can be packed into an empty head.

Karl Kraus, 1874–1936

My salad days, when I was green in judgment.

William Shakespeare, 1564–1616

Pocket all your knowledge with your watch and never pull it out in company unless desired.

Lord Philip Dormer Stanhope Chesterfield, 1694–1773

Nothing is more terrible than ignorance in action.

Johann Wolfgang von Goethe, 1749–1834

The radical invents the views. When he has worn them out, the conservative adopts them.

Mark Twain [Samuel Langhorne Clemens], 1835–1910

Solitude, the safeguard of mediocrity, is to genius the stern friend.

Ralph Waldo Emerson, 1803–1882

The stupid neither forgive nor forget; the naive forgive and forget; the wise forgive but do not forget.

Thomas Szasz, 1920–

It distresses me, this failure to keep pace with the leaders of thought, as they pass into oblivion.

Sir Max Beerbohm, 1872–1956

He who doesn't lose his wits over certain things has no wits to lose.

Gotthold Ephraim Lessing, 1729–1781

Little minds are interested in the extraordinary, great minds in the commonplace.

Elbert Hubbard, 1856–1915

Knowledge is little; to know the right context is much; to know the right spot is everything.

Hugo von Hofmannsthal, 1874–1929

A conclusion is the place where you got tired of thinking.

Arthur McBride Bloch, 1938–

Intuition becomes increasingly valuable in the new information society precisely because there is so much data.

John Naisbitt, 1929–

Applause is the spur of noble minds, the end and aim of weak ones.

Charles Caleb Colton, 1780–1832

Wear your learning, like your watch, in a private pocket; and do not pull it out and strike it, merely to show that you have one.

Lord Philip Dormer Stanhope Chesterfield, 1694–1773

There is no great genius without some touch of madness.

Lucius Annaeus Seneca, c. 4 B.C.–65 A.D.

There is a road from the eye to the heart that does not go through the intellect.

Gilbert Keith Chesterton, 1874–1936

How we hate this solemn Ego that accompanies the learned, like a double, wherever he goes.

Ralph Waldo Emerson, 1803–1882

I have found you an argument; I am not obliged to find you an understanding.

Dr. Samuel Johnson, 1709–1784

Deliberation is the work of many men. Action, of one alone.

Charles de Gaulle, 1890–1970

All that we know is nothing, we are merely crammed waste-paper baskets, unless we are in touch with that which laughs at all our knowing.

David Herbert Lawrence, 1885–1930

The greater the ignorance the greater the dogmatism.

Sir William Osler, 1849–1919

The knowledge of the world is only to be acquired in the world, and not in a closet.

Lord Philip Dormer Stanhope Chesterfield, 1694–1773

A proverb is one man's wit and all men's wisdom.

Bertrand Arthur William Russell, 1872–1970

He who has begun has half done. Dare to be wise; begin!

Horace [Quintus Horatius Flaccus], 65–8 B.C.

I prefer the errors of enthusiasm to the indifference of wisdom.

Anatole France [Jacques Anatole François Thibault], 1844–1924

How many pessimists end up by desiring the things they fear, in order to prove that they are right?

Robert Mallet, 1915–

Man's desires are limited by his perceptions; none can desire what he has not perceived.

William Blake, 1757–1827

7

Men, Women, and Relationships

Men, some to business, some to pleasure take; but ev'ry woman is at heart a rake.

Alexander Pope, 1688–1744

Behind every great man there is a great woman; and behind that woman is his wife.

Anonymous

Men who do not make advances to women are apt to become victims to women who make advances to them.

Walter Bagehot, 1826–1877

Women deserve to have more than twelve years between the ages of twenty-eight and forty.

James Thurber, 1894–1961

Most men who rail against women are railing at one woman only.

Remy de Gourmont, 1858–1915

Women are never stronger than when they arm themselves with their weakness.

Marie de Vichy-Chamrond, Marquise du Deffand, 1697–1780

Anybody who believes that the way to a man's heart is through his stomach flunked geography.

Robert Byrne, 1930–

It is assumed that the woman must wait, motionless, until she is wooed. That is how the spider waits for the fly.

George Bernard Shaw, 1856–1950

A happy home is one in which each spouse grants the possibility that the other may be right, though neither believes it.

Don Fraser, 1946–1985

Woman gives herself as a prize to the weak and as a prop to the strong, and no man ever has what he should.

Cesare Pavese, 1908–1950

As a rule, the person found out in a betrayal of love holds, all the same, the superior position of the two. It is the betrayed one who is humiliated.

Ada Leverson, 1865–1936

A kiss can be a comma, a question mark, or an exclamation point. That's a basic spelling that every woman should know.

Mistinguett [Jeanne Bourgeois], 1874–1956

Man's love is of man's life a thing apart; 'tis woman's whole existence.

George Noel Gordon, Lord Byron, 1788–1824

A beautiful woman should break her mirror early.

Baltasar Gracián, 1601–1658

He who loves the more is the inferior and must suffer.

Thomas Mann, 1875–1955

Before borrowing money from a friend, decide which you need most.

American proverb

A man who marries his mistress leaves a vacancy in that position.

Oscar Wilde, 1854–1900

True love is like ghosts, which everybody talks about and few have seen.

François, Duc de La Rochefoucauld, 1613–1680

Children begin by loving their parents. After a time they judge them. Rarely, if ever, do they forgive them.

Oscar Wilde, 1854–1900

In the misfortune of our friends, we find something which is not displeasing to us.

François, Duc de La Rochefoucauld, 1613–1680

Women prefer to talk in two's, while men prefer to talk in three's.

Gilbert Keith Chesterton, 1874–1936

In their first passion women love their lovers; in the others they love love.

François, Duc de La Rochefoucauld, 1613–1680

Love lodged in a woman's breast is but a guest.

Sir Henry Wotton, 1568–1639

Chaste men engender obscene literatures.

Decimus Maximus Ausonius, c. 310–395

The violence we do to ourselves in order to remain faithful to the one we love is hardly better than an act of infidelity.

François, Duc de La Rochefoucauld, 1613–1680

O, she is the antidote to desire.

William Congreve, 1670–1729

Anything will give up its secrets if you love it enough.

George Washington Carver, c. 1864–1943

To marry a second time represents the triumph of hope over experience.

Dr. Samuel Johnson, 1709–1784

A true friend is one who overlooks your failures and tolerates your successes.

Doug Larson, 1952–

On one issue at least, men and women agree; they both distrust women.

Henry Louis Mencken, 1880–1956

Who follows his wife in everything is an ignoramus.

The Talmud

Quarrels would not last long if the fault were only on one side.

François, Duc de La Rochefoucauld, 1613–1680

Women are the wild life of a country: Morality corresponds to game laws.

Anonymous

You never know till you try to reach them how accessible men are; but you must approach each man by the right door.

Henry Ward Beecher, 1813–1887

To cheat one's self out of love is the greatest deception of which there is no reparation in either time or eternity.

Søren Kierkegaard, 1813–1855

It is slavery and a disgrace if a wife supports her husband.

Anonymous

So heavy is the chain of wedlock that it needs two to carry it, and sometimes three.

Alexandre Dumas, fils 1824–1895

Do not rely completely on any other human being, however dear. We meet all life's greatest tests alone.

Agnes Campbell MacPhail, 1890–1954

Woman inspires us to great things, and prevents us from achieving them.

Alexandre Dumas

Scratch a lover and find a foe.

Dorothy Parker, 1893–1967

It takes a loose rein to keep a marriage tight.

John Stevenson

There is one who kisses, and the other who offers the cheek.

French proverb

What is irritating about love is that it is a crime that requires an accomplice.

Charles Baudelaire, 1821–1867

A relationship is what happens between two people who are waiting for something better to come along.

Anonymous

A woman who cannot be ugly is not beautiful.

Karl Kraus, 1874–1936

Once a woman has forgiven her man, she must not reheat his sins for breakfast.

Marlene Dietrich, 1904–1992

It is seldom indeed that one parts on good terms, because if one were on good terms one would not part.

Marcel Proust, 1871–1922

There can be no peace of mind in love, since the advantage one has secured is never anything but a fresh starting-point for further desires.

Marcel Proust, 1871–1922

In olden times sacrifices were made at the altar, a custom which is still continued.

Helen Rowland, 1875–1950

If a man hears much that a woman says, she is not beautiful.

Henry S. Haskins, 1878–1957

Marriage is the only war in which you sleep with the enemy.

François, Duc de La Rochefoucauld, 1613–1680

Take egotism out and you would castrate the benefactors.

Ralph Waldo Emerson, 1803–1882

You don't know a woman until you have had a letter from her.

Ada Leverson, 1865–1936

There are very few people who are not ashamed of having been in love when they no longer love each other.

François, Duc de La Rochefoucauld, 1613–1680

There are three important steps in a man's life: birth, marriage, and death
. . . but not necessarily in that order.

John M. Shanahan, 1939–

The females of all species are most dangerous when they appear to retreat.

Donald Robert Perry Marquis, 1878–1937

I will permit no man to narrow and degrade my soul by making me hate
him.

Booker Taliaferro Washington, 1856–1915

Men's vows are women's traitors.

William Shakespeare, 1564–1616

It would be impossible to "love" anyone or anything one knew
completely. Love is directed towards what lies hidden in its object.

Paul Valéry, 1871–1945

Every woman is wrong until she cries, and then she is right—instantly.

Sam Slick [Thomas Chandler Haliburton], 1796–1865

A man keeps another's secret better than he does his own. A woman, on the other hand, keeps her own better than another's.

Jean de La Bruyère, 1645–1695

Love is the whole history of a woman's life, it is but an episode in a man's.

Anne Louise Germaine de Staël, Barrone de Staël-Holstein
[Madame de Staël], 1766–1817

Men who cherish for women the highest respect are seldom popular with them.

Anonymous

Home life as we understand it is no more natural to us than a cage is natural to a cockatoo.

George Bernard Shaw, 1856–1950

A true friend is one who likes you despite your achievements.

Arnold Bennett, 1867–1931

As in political, so in literary action, a man wins friends for himself mostly by the passion of his prejudices.

Joseph Conrad, 1857–1924

It takes patience to appreciate domestic bliss; volatile spirits prefer unhappiness.

George Santayana, 1863–1952

That's the nature of women . . . not to love when we love them, and to love when we love them not.

Miguel de Cervantes, 1547–1616

It is because of men that women dislike one another.

Jean de La Bruyère, 1645–1695

When science discovers the center of the universe, a lot of people will be disappointed to find they are not it.

Bernard Baily, 1816–1902

There is no disguise which can for long conceal love where it exists or simulate it where it does not.

François, Duc de La Rochefoucauld, 1613–1680

Fame sometimes hath created something of nothing.

Thomas Fuller, 1608–1661

Marriage, *n.* The state or condition of a community consisting of a master, a mistress, and two slaves, making in all, two.

Ambrose Bierce, 1842–c. 1914

To have a good enemy, choose a friend: He knows where to strike.

Diane de Poitiers, Duchess de Valentinois, 1499–1566

Keep your eyes wide open before marriage, half shut afterwards.

Benjamin Franklin, 1706–1790

Everybody's friend is nobody's.

Arthur Schopenhauer, 1788–1860

Of all the icy blasts that blow on love, a request for money is the most chilling and havoc-wreaking.

Gustave Flaubert, 1821–1880

Never have a companion who casts you in the shade.

Baltasar Gracian, 1601–1658

It is better to be deceived by one's friends than to deceive them.

Johann Wolfgang von Goethe, 1749–1834

Jealousy is the great exaggerator.

Johann Christoph Friedrich von Schiller, 1775–1854

To be able to say how much you love is to love but little.

Petrarch [Francesco Petrarca], 1304–1374

Don't tell your friends their social faults; they will cure the fault and never forgive you.

Logan Pearsall Smith, 1865–1946

If all persons knew what they said of each other, there would not be four friends in the world.

Blaise Pascal, 1623–1662

Those who are faithful know only the trivial side of love; it is the faithless who know love's tragedies.

Oscar Wilde, 1854–1900

Love, and a cough, cannot be hid.

George Herbert, 1593–1633

What attracts us in a woman rarely binds us to her.

John Churton Collins, 1848–1908

Love built on beauty, soon as beauty, dies.

John Donne, 1572–1631

What men prize most is a privilege, even if it be that of chief mourner at a funeral.

James Russell Lowell, 1819–1891

The one charm of marriage is that it makes a life of deception absolutely necessary for both parties.

Oscar Wilde, 1854–1900

Where there's marriage without love, there will be love without marriage.

Benjamin Franklin, 1706–1790

Nothing spoils a romance so much as a sense of humor in the woman.

Oscar Wilde, 1854–1900

A woman we love rarely satisfies all our needs, and we deceive her with a woman whom we do not love.

Marcel Proust, 1871–1922

Beauty soon grows familiar to the lover, fades in his eye, and palls upon the sense.

Joseph Addison, 1672–1719

A wife is to thank God her husband hath faults. . . . A husband without faults is a dangerous observer.

George Savile, Marquess de Halifax, 1633–1695

Jealousy is always born with love, but does not always die with it.

François, Duc de La Rochefoucauld, 1613–1680

The big difference between sex for money and sex for free is that sex for money usually costs a lot less.

Brendan Behan, 1923–1964

If a friend tell thee a fault, imagine always that he telleth thee not the whole.

Thomas Fuller, 1608–1661

It's a sad house where the hen crows louder than the cock.

Scottish proverb

What a woman says to her ardent lover should be written in wind and running water.

Galius Valerius Catullus, 87–c. 54 B.C.

Adultery is the application of democracy to love.

Henry Louis Mencken, 1880–1956

It is a mistake to speak of a bad choice in love, since, as soon as a choice exists, it can only be bad.

Marcel Proust, 1871–1922

A man would create another man if one did not already exist, but a woman might live an eternity without even thinking of reproducing her own sex.

Johann Wolfgang von Goethe, 1749–1834

A man does not look behind the door unless he has stood there himself.

Henri Du Bois, 1863–1918

8

Religion, Nature, and God

He is a self-made man and worships his creator.

John Bright, 1811–1889

The only difference between the saint and the sinner is that every saint has a past, and every sinner has a future.

Oscar Wilde, 1854–1900

Be not deceived; God is not mocked: For whatsoever a man soweth, that shall he also reap.

Galatians 6:7

A God all mercy is a God unjust.

Edward Young, 1683–1765

Mercy but murders, pardoning those that kill.

William Shakespeare, 1564–1616

Are you not scared by seeing that the gypsies are more attractive to us than the apostles?

Ralph Waldo Emerson, 1803–1882

When the gods wish to punish us they answer our prayers.

Oscar Wilde, 1854–1900

Nothing emboldens sin so much as mercy.

William Shakespeare, 1564–1616

Men are not punished for their sins, but by them.

Elbert Hubbard, 1856–1915

God became man, granted. The devil became a woman.

Victor Hugo, 1802–1885

What men usually ask of God when they pray is that two and two not make four.

Anonymous

God made everything out of nothing. But the nothingness shows through.

Paul Valéry, 1871–1945

Science without religion is lame; religion without science is blind.

Albert Einstein, 1879–1955

Though the mills of God grind slowly; yet, they grind exceeding small.

Friedrich Von Logau, 1604–1655

Prayer does not change God, but it changes him who prays.

Søren Kierkegaard, 1813–1855

After your death you will be what you were before your birth.

Arthur Schopenhauer, 1788–1860

We have just enough religion to make us hate, but not enough to make us love one another.

Jonathan Swift, 1667–1745

There are few men who durst publish to the world the prayers they make to the Almighty God.

Michel Eyquem de Montaigne, 1533–1592

I never knew any man in my life who could not bear another's misfortunes perfectly like a Christian.

Alexander Pope, 1688–1744

Monkeys are superior to men in this: When a monkey looks into a mirror, he sees a monkey.

Malcolm de Chazal, 1902–1981

God does not pay weekly, but he pays at the end.

Dutch proverb

In nature, there are neither rewards nor punishments; there are consequences.

Robert Greene Ingersoll, 1833–1899

To one who has faith, no explanation is necessary. To one without faith, no explanation is possible.

Saint Thomas Aquinas, 1225–1274

By night, an atheist half believes in God.

Edward Young, 1683–1765

Most men's anger about religion is as if two men should quarrel for a lady that neither of them care for.

George Savile, Marquess de Halifax, 1633–1695

Ethical man: A Christian holding four aces.

Mark Twain [Samuel Langhorne Clemens], 1835–1910

Faith which does not doubt is dead faith.

Miguel de Unamuno, 1864–1936

Repetition is the only form of permanence that nature can achieve.

George Santayana, 1863–1952

Nothing ever gets anywhere. The earth keeps turning round and gets nowhere. The moment is the only thing that counts.

Jean Cocteau, 1889–1963

Whoever obeys the gods, to him they particularly listen.

Homer, c. 700 B.C.

Personal sin reflected upon breeds compassion.

John M. Shanahan, 1939–

Every sect is a moral check on its neighbor. Competition is as wholesome in religion as in commerce.

Walter Savage Landor, 1775–1864

Can one be a saint if God does not exist? That is the only concrete problem I know of today.

Albert Camus, 1913–1960

Make me chaste and continent, but not just yet.

Saint Augustine, 354–430

To what excesses will men not go for the sake of a religion in which they believe so little and which they practice so imperfectly!

Jean de La Bruyère, 1645–1695

The cistern contains: The fountain overflows.

William Blake, 1757–1827

Martyrs create faith, faith does not create martyrs.

Miguel de Unamuno, 1864–1936

In a small house God has His corner; in a big house, He has to stand in the hall.

Swedish proverb

Indeed, I tremble for my country when I reflect that God is just.

Thomas Jefferson, 1743–1826

It is much easier to repent of sins that we have committed than to repent of those we intend to commit.

Josh Billings [Henry Wheeler Shaw], 1818–1885

A man with God is always in the majority.

John Knox, c. 1513–1572

The devil's boots don't creak.

Scottish proverb

Mathematics is the only science where one never knows what one is talking about nor whether what is said is true.

Bertrand Arthur William Russell, 1872–1970

Life is the art of drawing sufficient conclusions from insufficient premises.

Samuel Butler, 1835–1902

Wherever a man may happen to turn, whatever a man may undertake, he will always end up by returning to that path which nature has marked out for him.

Johann Wolfgang von Goethe, 1749–1834

All progress is based upon a universal, innate desire on the part of every organism to live beyond its income.

Samuel Butler, 1835–1902

9

Life's Passages

We are linked by blood, and blood is memory without language.

Joyce Carol Oates, 1938–

A ship in harbor is safe—but that is not what ships are for.

John A. Shedd, 1859–c. 1928

Be on your guard against a silent dog and still water.

Latin proverb

Never mistake knowledge for wisdom. One helps you make a living; the other helps you make a life.

Sandra Carey, 1941–

While grief is fresh, every attempt to divert it only irritates.

Dr. Samuel Johnson, 1709–1784

Conscience and cowardice are really the same things.

Oscar Wilde, 1854–1900

Life contains but two tragedies. One is not to get your heart's desire; the other is to get it.

George Bernard Shaw, 1856–1950

Life is so constructed, that the event does not, cannot, will not, match the expectation.

Charlotte Brontë, 1816–1855

Who so neglects learning in his youth, loses the past and is dead for the future.

Euripides, 485–406 B.C.

A hen is only an egg's way of making another egg.

Samuel Butler, 1835–1902

Luck never gives; it only lends.

Swedish proverb

Oh, what a bitter thing it is to look into happiness through another man's eyes.

William Shakespeare, 1564–1616

Nothing is a stronger influence psychologically on their environment, and especially on their children, than the unlived lives of the parents.

Carl Gustav Jung, 1875–1961

The chief mourner does not always attend the funeral.

Ralph Waldo Emerson, 1803–1882

Children are the living messages we send to a time we will not see.

Neil Postman, 1931–

Experience is what you get when you didn't get what you wanted.

Italian proverb

Success is how high you bounce when you hit bottom.

George Smith Patton, 1885–1945

Children have never been good at listening to their elders, but they have never failed to imitate them.

James Baldwin, 1924–1987

You don't have to deserve your mother's love. You have to deserve your father's. He's more particular.

Robert Frost, 1874–1963

Poverty sits by the cradle of all our great men and rocks all of them to manhood.

Heinrich Heine, 1797–1856

It's going to be fun to watch and see how long the meek can keep the earth after they inherit it.

Frank McKinney "Kin" Hubbard, 1868–1930

It is an easy matter for a stingy man to get rich—but what's the use?

American proverb

I have not been afraid of excess: Excess on occasion is exhilarating. It prevents moderation from acquiring the deadening effect of a habit.

William Somerset Maugham, 1874–1965

Every man thinks meanly of himself for not having been a soldier, or not having been to sea.

Dr. Samuel Johnson, 1709–1784

He that falls by himself never cries.

Turkish proverb

How sharper than a serpent's tooth it is to have a thankless child.

William Shakespeare, 1564–1616

Death is nothing to us, since when we are, death has not come, and when death has come, we are not.

Epicurus, 341–270 B.C.

The best-educated human being is the one who understands most about the life in which he is placed.

Helen Keller, 1880–1968

The fear of death is more to be dreaded than death itself.

Publilius Syrus, first century B.C.

What was silent in the father speaks in the son, and often I found in the son the unveiled secret of the father.

Friedrich Wilhelm Nietzsche, 1844–1900

The wise person questions himself, the fool others.

Henri Arnold, 1918

Cruel is the strife of brothers.

Aristotle, 384–322 B.C.

Don't limit a child to your own learning, for he was born in another time.

Anonymous

There is no cure for birth and death, save to enjoy the interval.

George Santayana, 1863–1952

Man will do many things to get himself loved; he will do all things to get himself envied.

Mark Twain [Samuel Langhorne Clemens], 1835–1910

He that hath wife and children hath given hostages to fortune; for they are impediments to great enterprises, either of virtue or mischief.

Sir Francis Bacon, 1561–1626

He that has no fools, knaves, nor beggars in his family was begot by a flash of lightning.

Thomas Fuller, 1654–1734

We rarely find anyone who can say he has lived a happy life, and who, content with his life, can return from the world like a satisfied guest.

Horace [Quintus Horatius Flaccus], 65–83 B.C.

We frequently forgive those who bore us, but cannot forgive those whom we bore.

François, Duc de La Rochefoucauld, 1613–1680

All the world is competent to judge my pictures except those who are of my profession.

William Hogarth, 1697–1764

Luck is a matter of preparation meeting opportunity.

Oprah Winfrey, 1953–

Equality is what does not exist among mortals.

e. e. cummings, 1894–1962

Men are what their mothers made them.

Ralph Waldo Emerson, 1803–1882

Human beings cling to their delicious tyrannies and to their exquisite nonsense, till death stares them in the face.

Sydney Smith, 1771–1845

A father is a banker provided by nature.

Anonymous

Young men think old men are fools; but old men know young men are fools.

George Chapman, c. 1559–1634

If a man once fall, all will tread upon him.

Thomas Fuller, 1654–1734

Three generations from shirtsleeves to shirtsleeves.

Andrew Carnegie, 1835–1919

Learning music by reading about it is like making love by mail.

Luciano Pavarotti, 1935–

The joys of parents are secret, and so are their griefs and fears.

Sir Francis Bacon, 1561–1626

My best creation is my children.

Diane von Furstenberg, 1946–

One short sleep past, we wake eternally, and death shall be no more; death, thou shalt die.

John Donne, 1572–1631

The scalded dog fears hot water, and afterwards, cold.

Italian proverb

Power corrupts the few, while weakness corrupts the many.

Eric Hoffer, 1902–1983

I have learned to use the word impossible with the greatest caution.

Wernher von Braun, 1912–1977

For rarely are sons similar to their fathers; most are worse, and a few are better than their fathers.

Homer, c. 700 B.C.

He that has satisfied his thirst turns his back on the well.

Baltasar Gracian, 1601–1658

The tragedy of old age is not that one is old, but that one is young.

Oscar Wilde, 1854–1900

Children's talent to endure stems from their ignorance of alternatives.

Maya Angelou, 1928–

All women become like their mothers. That is their tragedy. No man does. That's his.

Oscar Wilde, 1854–1900

The poor man's wisdom is despised and his words are not heard.

Ecclesiastes 9:16

To weep is to make less the depth of grief.

William Shakespeare, 1564–1616

The deepest definition of youth is life as yet untouched by tragedy.

Alfred North Whitehead, 1861–1947

Who doesn't desire his father's death?

Fedor Dostoevsky, 1821–1881

During the first period of a man's life the greatest danger is not to take the risk.

Søren Kierkegaard, 1813–1855

There is a mercy which is weakness, and even treason against the common good.

George Eliot [Marian Evans Cross], 1819–1880

Fame is the thirst of youth.

George Noel Gordon, Lord Byron, 1788–1824

As a well-spent day brings happy sleep, so a life well used brings happy death.

Leonardo da Vinci, 1452–1519

It is always self-defeating to pretend to the style of a generation younger than your own; it simply erases your own experience in history.

Renata Adler, 1938–

Problems are messages.

Shakti Gawain, 1948–

The affection of a father and a son are different: The father loves the person of the son, and the son loves the memory of his father.

Anonymous

Wisdom consists of the anticipation of consequences.

Norman Cousins, 1912–1990

Children begin by loving their parents; as they grow older they judge them; sometimes they forgive them.

Oscar Wilde, 1854–1900

Do well and you will have no need of ancestors.

Voltaire [François Marie Arouet], 1694–1778

Greatness of name, in the father, ofttimes helps not forth, but overwhelms the son: They stand too near one another. The shadow kills the growth.

Ben Jonson, c. 1573–1637

A short saying oft contains much wisdom.

Sophocles, c. 495–406 B.C.

That sign of old age, extolling the past at the expense of the present.

Sydney Smith, 1771–1845.

The most important thing that parents can teach their children is how to get along without them.

Frank A. Clark, 1911

The young have aspirations that never come to pass, the old have reminiscences of what never happened.

Saki [Hector Hugo Monro], 1870–1916

There is no refuge from confession but suicide; and suicide is confession.

Daniel Webster, 1782–1852

Fear is the parent of cruelty.

James Anthony Froude, 1818–1894

The difference between us is that my family begins with me, whereas yours ends with you.

Iphicrates, c. 419–348 B.C.

The deeper the sorrow the less tongue it hath.

The Talmud

Happiness is beneficial for the body but it is grief that develops the powers of the mind.

Marcel Proust, 1871–1922

Truth always originates in a minority of one, and every custom begins as a broken precedent.

William J. Durant, 1885–1981

When we are born, we cry that we are come to this great stage of fools.

William Shakespeare, 1564–1616

Ah, if the rich were rich as the poor fancy riches.

Ralph Waldo Emerson, 1803–1882

There is only one success—to be able to spend your life in your own way.

Christopher Morley, 1890–1957

If one could recover the uncompromising spirit of one's youth, one's greatest indignation would be for what one has become.

André Gide, 1869–1951

Women run to extremes; they are either better or worse than men.

Jean de La Bruyère, 1645–1695

You cannot do a kindness too soon, for you never know how soon it will be too late.

Ralph Waldo Emerson, 1803–1882

A rich man is either a scoundrel or the heir of a scoundrel.

Spanish proverb

Death is a distant rumor to the young.

Andrew A. Rooney, 1919–

The test of a man or woman's breeding is how they behave in a quarrel.

George Bernard Shaw, 1856–1950

It is better to waste one's youth than to do nothing with it at all.

Georges Courteline, 1860–1929

Happy families are all alike; every unhappy family is unhappy in its own way.

Leo Nikolaevich Tolstoy, 1828–1911

It is only rarely that one can see in a little boy the promise of a man, but one can almost always see in a little girl the threat of a woman.

Alexandre Dumas, fils 1824–1895

Not by age but by capacity is wisdom acquired.

Titus Maccius Plautus, 254–184 B.C.

Crime expands according to our willingness to put up with it.

Barry Farber, 1947–

Old age is the most unexpected of all the things that happen to a man.

Leon Trotsky [Lev Davidovich Bronstein], 1879–1940

Diogenes struck the father when the son swore.

Robert Burton, 1577–1640

Self-love, my liege, is not so vile a sin as self-neglecting.

William Shakespeare, 1564–1616

Everything bows to success, even grammar.

Victor Hugo, 1802–1885

Death twitches my ear. "Live," he says; "I am coming."

Virgil [Publius Vergilius Maro], 70–19 B.C.

Every parent is at some time the father of the unreturned prodigal, with nothing to do but keep his house open to hope.

John Anthony Ciardi, 1916–1986

Sometimes the best way to convince someone he is wrong is to let him have his way.

Red O'Donnell, c. 1900–1984

Old and young, we are all on our last cruise.

Robert Louis Stevenson, 1850–1894

When sorrows come, they come not as single spies, but in battalions!

William Shakespeare, 1564–1616

Life is a festival only to the wise.

Ralph Waldo Emerson, 1803–1882

The closer to the truth, the closer to the nerve.

John M. Shanahan, 1939–

Never tell people how to do things. Tell them what to do and they will surprise you with their ingenuity.

George Smith Patton, 1885–1945

Age is no better, hardly so well, qualified for an instructor as youth, for it has not profited so much as it has lost.

Henry David Thoreau, 1817–1862

Pay attention to your enemies, for they are the first to discover your mistakes.

Antisthenes, c. 445–c. 365 B.C.

Misery acquaints a man with strange bedfellows.

William Shakespeare, 1564–1616

Most men make use of the first part of their life to render the last part miserable.

Jean de La Bruyère, 1645–1695

Our enemies approach nearer to truth in their judgments of us than we do ourselves.

François, Duc de La Rochefoucauld, 1613–1680

Learn to say no. It will be of more use to you than to be able to read Latin.

Charles Haddon Spurgeon, 1834–1892

By protracting life, we do not deduct one jot from the duration of death.

Lucretius [Tirus Lucretius Carus], 99–55 B.C.

There is no more fatal blunder than he who consumes the greater part of his life getting his living.

Henry David Thoreau, 1817–1862

The small demerit extinguishes a long service.

Thomas Fuller, 1654–1734

One-half of the troubles of this life can be traced to saying yes too quickly and not saying no soon enough.

Josh Billings [Henry Wheeler Shaw], 1818–1885

We are always paid for our suspicion by finding what we suspect.

Henry David Thoreau, 1817–1862

10

Human Foibles

A stiff apology is a second insult.

Gilbert Keith Chesterton, 1874–1936

We judge ourselves by what we feel capable of doing, while others judge us by what we have already done.

Henry Wadsworth Longfellow, 1807–1882

You raise your voice when you should reinforce your argument.

Dr. Samuel Johnson, 1709–1784

Skating on thin ice is better than skating on no ice at all.

John M. Shanahan, 1939–

There is a time for departure even when there's no certain place to go.

Tennessee Williams [Thomas Lanier], 1911–1983

An endeavor to please elders is at the bottom of high marks and mediocre careers.

John Jay Chapman, 1862–1933

Decide promptly, but never give any reasons. Your decisions may be right, but your reasons are sure to be wrong.

Lord William Murray Mansfield, 1705–1793

Idealism increases in direct proportion to one's distance from the problem.

John Galsworthy, 1867–1933

A positive attitude may not solve all your problems, but it will annoy enough people to make it worth the effort.

Herm Albright, 1876–1944

The man who leaves money to charity in his will is only giving away what no longer belongs to him.

Voltaire [François Marie Arouet], 1694–1778

Philosophy: A route of many roads leading from nowhere to nothing.

Ambrose Bierce, 1842–c. 1914

My life is in the hands of any fool who makes me lose my temper.

Joseph Hunter, 1914–1974

Don't sing for me, dance for me.

Anonymous

Violence is the last refuge of the incompetent.

Isaac Asimov, 1920–1992

Deadlines are the mothers of invention.

John M. Shanahan, 1939–

To exaggerate is to weaken.

Jean François de La Harpe, 1739–1803

Most people have seen worse things in private than they pretend to be shocked at in public.

Edgar Watson Howe, 1853–1937

You are permitted in time of great danger to walk with the devil until you have crossed the bridge.

Bulgarian proverb

Courage is resistance to fear, mastery of fear, not absence of fear.

Mark Twain [Samuel Langhorne Clemens], 1835–1910

If we had no faults of our own, we would not take so much pleasure in noticing those of others.

François, Duc de La Rochefoucauld, 1613–1680

Until the day of his death, no man can be sure of his courage.

Jean Anouilh, 1910–1987

Anger as soon as fed is dead—'Tis starving makes it fat.

Emily Dickinson, 1830–1886

Do not free a camel of the burden of his hump; you may be freeing him from being a camel.

Gilbert Keith Chesterton, 1874–1936

Men can acquire knowledge but not wisdom. Some of the greatest fools ever known were learned men.

Spanish proverb

The only way to get rid of a temptation is to yield to it.

Oscar Wilde, 1854–1900

It is better to wear out one's shoes than one's sheets.

Genoese proverb

No person was ever honored for what he received. Honor has been the reward for what he gave.

Calvin Coolidge, 1872–1933

Living movements do not come of committees.

Cardinal John Henry Newman, 1801–1890

Without the aid of prejudice and custom, I should not be able to find my way across the room.

William Hazlitt, 1778–1830

There is no such thing as a great talent without great will-power.

Honoré de Balzac, 1799–1850

All affectation is the vain and ridiculous attempt of poverty to appear rich.

Johann Kasper Lavater, 1741–1801

I do not believe in a fate that falls on men however they act; but I do not believe in a fate that falls on men unless they act.

Gilbert Keith Chesterton, 1874–1936

The mass of men lead lives of quiet desperation.

Henry David Thoreau, 1817–1862

In this world there are only two tragedies. One is not getting what one wants, and the other is getting it.

Oscar Wilde, 1854–1900

Beware the tyranny of the minority.

Latin proverb

Lazy people are always looking for something to do.

Luc de Clapiers de Vauvenargues, 1715–1747

The time is always right to do what is right.

Martin Luther King, Jr., 1929–1968

A man who has to be convinced to act before he acts is not a man of action. . . . You must act as you breathe.

Georges Clemenceau, 1841–1929

The efforts which we make to escape from our destiny only serve to lead us into it.

Ralph Waldo Emerson, 1803–1882

Luck is being ready for the chance.

James Frank Dobie, 1888–1964

Nothing arouses ambition so much . . . as the trumpet clang of another's fame.

Baltasar Gracian, 1601–1658

The arm of the moral universe is long, but it bends toward justice.

Martin Luther King Jr., 1929–1968

The only difference between a caprice and a lifelong passion is that the caprice lasts a little longer.

Oscar Wilde, 1854–1900

In things pertaining to enthusiasm, no man is sane who does not know how to be insane on proper occasions.

Henry Ward Beecher, 1813–1887

Inferiors revolt in order that they may be equal, and equals that they may be superior. Such is the state of mind which creates revolutions.

Aristotle, 384–322 B.C.

The secret of all victory lies in the organization of the non-obvious.

Oswald Spengler, 1880–1936

No profit grows where is no pleasure taken; in brief, sir, study what you most affect.

William Shakespeare, 1564–1616

Unless a man has trained himself for his chance, the chance will only make him ridiculous.

William Matthews, 1942–1997

Never forget what a man says to you when he is angry.

Henry Ward Beecher, 1813–1887

In skating over thin ice, our safety is in our speed.

Ralph Waldo Emerson, 1803–1882

Fortunately for serious minds, a bias recognized is a bias sterilized.

A. Eustace Haydon, 1880–1975

The worst thing about some men is that when they are not drunk they are sober.

William Butler Yeats, 1865–1939

We may affirm absolutely that nothing great in the world has been accomplished without passion.

Georg Wilhelm Friedrich Hegel, 1770–1831

Nothing except a battle lost can be half so melancholy as a battle won.

Arthur Wellesley, Duke of Wellington, 1769–1852

Many become brave when brought to bay.

Norwegian proverb

Dare to do things worthy of imprisonment if you mean to be of consequence.

Juvenal [Decimus Junius Juvenalis], c. 55–c. 130

Mishaps are like knives, that either serve us or cut us, as we grasp them by the blade or the handle.

James Russell Lowell, 1819–1891

A practical man is a man who practices the errors of his forefathers.

Benjamin Disraeli, Earl of Beaconsfield, 1804–1881

Liberty means responsibility. That is why most men dread it.

George Bernard Shaw, 1856–1950

Wherever I sit is the head of the table.

Henry Louis Mencken, 1880–1956

Those who mistake their good luck for their merit are inevitably bound for disaster.

Christopher J. Herold, 1919–1964

Consensus is the negation of leadership.

Margaret Thatcher [Hilda Roberts], 1925–

Envy's a sharper spur than pay.

John Gay, 1685–1732

For a man to achieve all that is demanded of him he must regard himself as greater than he is.

Johann Wolfgang von Goethe, 1749–1834

The man who dies rich . . . dies disgraced.

Andrew Carnegie, 1835–1919

Prejudice is the child of ignorance.

William Hazlitt, 1778–1830

Passion and prejudice govern the world; only under the name of reason.

John Wesley, 1703–1791

If you wish to drown, do not torture yourself with shallow water.

Bulgarian proverb

Opportunity is sometimes hard to recognize if you're only looking for a lucky break.

Monta Crane

Chance is always powerful. Let your hook be always cast; in the pool where you least expect it, there will be a fish.

Ovid [Publius Ovidius Naso], 43 B.C.–18 A.D.

Few things help an individual more than to place responsibility upon him and to let him know that you trust him.

Booker Taliaferro Washington, 1856–1915

He that leaveth nothing to chance will do few things ill, but he will do very few things.

George Savile, Marquess de Halifax, 1633–1695

Let all the learned say what they can, 'tis ready money makes the man.

William Somerville, 1675–1742

If you hate a person, you hate something in him that is part of yourself. What isn't part of ourselves doesn't disturb us.

Herman Hesse, 1877–1962

"Why not" is a slogan for an interesting life.

Mason Cooley

Opportunity's favorite disguise is trouble.

Frank Tyger

Fortune favors the brave.

Virgil [Publius Vergilius Maro], 70–19 B.C.

No great man ever complains of want of opportunity.

Ralph Waldo Emerson, 1803–1882

You don't hold your own in the world by standing on guard, but by attacking and getting well hammered yourself.

George Bernard Shaw, 1856–1950

Our doubts are traitors, and make us lose the good we oft might win, by fearing to attempt.

William Shakespeare, 1564–1616

That old law about "an eye for an eye" leaves everybody blind.

Martin Luther King, Jr., 1929–1968

Jealousy, that dragon which slays love under the pretense of keeping it alive.

Havelock Ellis, 1859–1939

Wherever we look upon this earth, the opportunities take shape within the problems.

Nelson Rockefeller, 1908–1979

Growth demands a temporary surrender of security.

Gail Sheehy, 1937–

Now he'll outstare the lightning. To be furious, is to be frighted out of fear.

William Shakespeare, 1564–1616

Life shrinks or expands in proportion to one's courage.

Anaïs Nin, 1903–1977

He that wrestles with us strengthens our nerves, and sharpens our skill. Our antagonist is our helper.

Edmund Burke, 1729–1797

There is no passion so much transports the sincerity of judgment as doth anger.

Michel Eyquem de Montaigne, 1533–1592

Courage is fear holding on a minute longer.

George Smith Patton, 1885–1945

There is never jealousy where there is not strong regard.

Washington Irving, 1783–1859

A certain amount of opposition is a great help to a man. Kites rise against, not with the wind.

John Neal, 1793–1876

Courage is doing what you're afraid to do. There can be no courage unless you're scared.

Edward Vernon Rickenbacker, 1890–1973

Only the brave know how to forgive. . . . A coward never forgave; it is not in his nature.

Laurence Sterne, 1713–1768

When we ask advice we are usually looking for an accomplice.

Charles Varlet de La Grange, 1639–1692

Eyes are more accurate witnesses than ears.

Heraclitus, c. 540–c. 480 B.C.

One man with courage makes a majority.

Attributed to Andrew Jackson, 1767–1845

The concessions of the weak are the concessions of fear.

Edmund Burke, 1729–1797

Except a person be part coward, it is not a compliment to say he is brave.

Mark Twain [Samuel Langhorne Clemens], 1835–1910

We'll have a swashing and a martial outside, as many other mannish cowards have.

William Shakespeare, 1564–1616

The man who can't dance thinks the band is no good.

Polish proverb

A great part of courage is the courage of having done the thing before.

Ralph Waldo Emerson, 1803–1882

Nobody speaks the truth when there's something they must have.

Elizabeth Dorothea Cole Bowen, 1899–1973

In our way we were both snobs, and no snob welcomes another who has risen with him.

Sir Cecil Walter Hardy Beaton, 1904–1980

Everyone is a prisoner of his own experiences. No one can eliminate prejudices—just recognize them.

Edward Roscoe Murrow, 1908–1965

The only interesting answers are those which destroy the questions.

Susan Sontag, 1933–

All my best thoughts were stolen by the ancients.

Ralph Waldo Emerson, 1803–1882

Heaven has no rage like love to hatred turned nor hell a fury like a woman scorned.

William Congreve, 1670–1729

We often give our enemies the means for our own destruction.

Aesop, c. 550 B.C.

When you teach your son, you teach your son's son.

The Talmud

Who overcomes by force hath overcome but half his foe.

John Milton, 1608–1674

Kill a man, and you are a murderer. Kill millions of men, and you are a conqueror. Kill everyone and you are a god.

Jean Rostand, 1894–1977

He who mistrusts most should be trusted least.

Theognis, c. 545 B.C.

11

Pursuits—Artistic and Otherwise

Artistic temperament is a disease that afflicts amateurs.

Gilbert Keith Chesterton, 1874–1936

The great American novel has not only already been written, it has already been rejected.

Frank Dane

Few great men could pass Personnel.

Paul Goodman, 1911–1972

And the trouble is, if you don't risk anything, you risk even more.

Erica Jong, 1942–

The world's great men have not commonly been great scholars, nor great scholars great men.

Oliver W. Holmes Sr., 1806–1894

"For example" is not proof.

Yiddish proverb

Let early education be a sort of amusement; you will then be better able to find out the natural bent.

Plato, c. 428–348 B.C.

Devotees of grammatical studies have not been distinguished for any very remarkable felicities of expression.

Bronson Alcott, 1799–1888

Luck is infatuated with the efficient.

Persian proverb

When two men in business always agree, one of them is unnecessary.

William Wrigley Jr., 1861–1932

Whenever you see a successful business, someone once made a courageous decision.

Peter Drucker, 1909–

Avoid, as you would the plague, a clergyman who is also a man of business.

Saint Jerome, c. 342–420

If you're strong enough, there are no precedents.

Francis Scott Key Fitzgerald, 1896–1940

Everyone has a talent; what is rare is the courage to follow the talent to the dark place where it leads.

Erica Jong, 1942–

One must not always think that feeling is everything. Art is nothing without form.

Gustave Flaubert, 1821–1880

I think it's bad to talk about one's present work, for it spoils something at the root of the creative act. It discharges the tension.

Norman Mailer, 1923–

In any evolutionary process, even in the arts, the search for novelty becomes corrupting.

Kenneth Ewart Boulding, 1910–1993

No matter how well you perform there's always somebody of intelligent opinion who thinks it's lousy.

Laurence Olivier, Baron Olivier of Brighton, 1907–1989

What I like in a good author is not what he says, but what he whispers.

Logan Pearsall Smith, 1865–1946

I hear much of people's calling out to punish the guilty, but very few are concerned to clear the innocent.

Daniel Defoe, 1660–1731

You can't wait for inspiration. You have to go after it with a club.

Jack London [John Griffith], 1896–1916

Man exploits man. Under communism, it's just the opposite.

Russian saying

A life being very short, and the quiet hours of it few, we ought to waste none of them in reading valueless books.

John Ruskin, 1819–1900

Mediocre men often have the most acquired knowledge.

Claude Bernard, 1813–1878

The man who has never been flogged has never been taught.

Menander of Athens, c. 342–292 B.C.

Reading means borrowing.

Georg Christoph Lichtenberg, 1742–1799

Deep vers'd in books and shallow in himself.

John Milton, 1608–1674

Books bear him up a while, and make him try to swim with bladders of philosophy.

John Wilmot, Earl of Rochester, 1647–1680

If poverty is the mother of crime, stupidity is its father.

Jean de La Bruyère, 1645–1695

It is better to be a mouse in a cat's mouth than a man in a lawyer's hands.

Spanish proverb

But desire of knowledge, like the thirst of riches, increases ever with the acquisition of it.

Laurence Sterne, 1713–1768

The investigation of the meaning of words is the beginning of education.

Antisthenes, c. 445–c. 365 B.C.

Men in business are in as much danger from those at work under them as from those that work against them.

George Savile, Marquess de Halifax, 1633–1695

What does not destroy me, makes me stronger.

Friedrich Wilhelm Nietzsche, 1844–1900

Educated men are as much superior to uneducated men as the living are to the dead.

Aristotle, 384–322 B.C.

When a thing ceases to be a subject of controversy, it ceases to be a subject of interest.

William Hazlitt, 1778–1830

Education makes a people easy to lead, but difficult to drive; easy to govern but impossible to enslave.

Baron Henry Peter Brougham, 1778–1868

Some for renown, on scraps of learning dote, and think they grow immortal as they quote.

Edward Young, 1683–1765

Reading maketh a full man, conference a ready man, and writing an exact man.

Sir Francis Bacon, 1561–1626

Acting is therefore the lowest of the arts, if it is an art at all.

George Moore, 1852–1933

Genius . . . means little more than the faculty of perceiving in an unhabitual way.

William James, 1842–1910

Executive ability is deciding quickly and getting somebody else to do the work.

J. G. Pollard, 1871–1937

Learning hath gained most by those books by which the printers have lost.

Thomas Fuller, 1608–1661

About the most originality that any writer can hope to achieve honestly is to steal with good judgment.

Josh Billings [Henry Wheeler Shaw], 1818–1885

Nothing is so good as it seems beforehand.

George Eliot [Marian Evans Cross], 1819–1880

There are moments when everything goes well; don't be frightened, it won't last.

Jules Renard, 1864–1910

Whatever their other contributions to our society, lawyers could be an important source of protein.

Guindon cartoon caption

Crime is a logical extension of the sort of behavior that is often considered perfectly respectable in legitimate business.

Robert Rice, 1916–

An actor is something less than a man, while an actress is something more than a woman.

Richard Burton, 1925–1984

There be some men are born only to suck out the poison of books.

Ben Jonson, c. 1573–1637

The price one pays for pursuing any profession or calling is an intimate knowledge of its ugly side.

James Baldwin, 1924–1987

What it lies in our power to do, it lies in our power not to do.

Aristotle, 384–322 B.C.

A criminal is a person with predatory instincts who has not sufficient capital to form a corporation.

Howard Scott, 1926–

A work settles nothing, just as the labor of a whole generation settles nothing. Sons, and the morrow, always start afresh.

Cesare Pavese, 1908–1950

A decision is the action an executive must take when he has information · so incomplete that the answer does not suggest itself.

Arthur William Radford, 1896–1973

Men of genius do not excel in any profession because they labor in it, but they labor in it because they excel.

William Hazlitt, 1778–1830

A professor is one who talks in someone else's sleep.

W. H. Auden, 1907–1973

The cleverly expressed opposite of any generally accepted idea is worth a fortune to somebody.

Francis Scott Key Fitzgerald, 1896–1940

If a little knowledge is dangerous, where is the man who has so much as to be out of danger?

Thomas Henry Huxley, 1825–1895

Those who can, do; those who can't, teach; and those who can do neither, administer.

Collet Calverley

A committee is a cul-de-sac down which ideas are lured and then quietly strangled.

Barnett Cocks, 1907–1989

Every single instance of a friend's insincerity increases our dependence on the efficacy of money.

William Shenstone, 1714–1763

Ambition drove many men to become false; to have one thought locked in the breast, another ready on the tongue.

Sallust [Gaius Sallustius Crispus], 86–34 B.C.

The secret of business is to know something that nobody else knows.

Aristotle Onassis, 1900–1975

Necessity never made a good bargain.

Benjamin Franklin, 1706–1790

Perpetual devotion to what a man calls his business, is only to be sustained by perpetual neglect of many other things.

Robert Louis Stevenson, 1850–1894

Look wise, say nothing, and grunt. Speech was given to conceal thought.

Sir William Osler, 1849–1919

There is no work of art that is without short cuts.

André Gide, 1869–1951

Constant popping off of proverbs will make thee a byword thyself.

Thomas Fuller, 1608–1661

You had better be a round peg in a square hole than a square peg in a square hole. The latter is in for life, while the first is only an indeterminate sentence.

Elbert Hubbard, 1856–1915

A work should contain its total meaning within itself and should impress it on the spectator before he even knows the subject.

Henri Matisse, 1869–1954

A book calls for pen, ink, and a writing desk; today the rule is that pen, ink, and a writing desk call for a book.

Friedrich Wilhelm Nietzsche, 1844–1900

A man really writes for an audience of about ten persons. Of course if others like it, that is clear gain. But if those ten are satisfied, he is content.

Alfred North Whitehead, 1861–1947

You know who the critics are? The men who have failed in literature and art.

Benjamin Disraeli, Earl of Beaconsfield, 1804–1881

Speech is the small change of silence.

George Meredith, 1828–1909

Originality does not consist in saying what no one has ever said before, but in saying exactly what you think yourself.

James Fitzjames Stephen, 1859–1892

The creative mind plays with the objects it loves.

Carl Gustav Jung, 1875–1961

The artist doesn't see things as they are, but as he is.

Anonymous

If you can find a path with no obstacles, it probably doesn't lead anywhere.

Frank A. Clark, 1911–

It is worse still to be ignorant of your ignorance.

Saint Jerome, c. 342–420

When some passion or effect is described in a natural style, we find within ourselves the truth of what we hear, without knowing it was there.

Blaise Pascal, 1623–1662

The difference between the right word and the almost right word is the difference between lightning and the lightning bug.

Mark Twain [Samuel Langhorne Clemens], 1835–1910

Imitation is criticism.

William Blake, 1757–1827

At least half the mystery novels published violate the law that the solution, once revealed, must seem to be inevitable.

Raymond Chandler, 1888–1959

Most editors are failed writers—but so are most writers.

Thomas Stearns Eliot, 1888–1965

To justify our likes and dislikes, we generally say that the work we dislike is not serious.

Walter Richard Sickert, 1860–1942

If your ship doesn't come in, swim out to it!

Jonathan Winters, 1925–

Be regular and orderly in your life like a bourgeois, so that you may be violent and original in your work.

Gustave Flaubert, 1821–1880

No author is a man of genius to his publisher.

Attributed to Heinrich Heine, 1797–1856

An excellent precept for writers: Have a clear idea of all the phrases and expressions you need, and you will find them.

Ximenes Doudan, 1800–1872

The luck of having talent is not enough; one must also have a talent for luck.

Louis Hector Berlioz, 1803–1869

Reading is sometimes an ingenious device for avoiding thought.

Sir Arthur Helps, 1813–1875

Would you persuade, speak of interest, not of reason.

Benjamin Franklin, 1706–1790

The artist who is not also a craftsman is no good; but, alas, most of our artists are nothing else.

Johann Wolfgang von Goethe, 1749–1834

Just get it down on paper, and then we'll see what to do with it.

Maxwell Evarts Perkins, 1884–1947

Only a person with a Best Seller mind can write Best Sellers.

Aldous Leonard Huxley, 1894–1963

For art to exist, for any sort of aesthetic activity or perception to exist, a certain physiological precondition is indispensable: intoxication.

Friedrich Wilhelm Nietzsche, 1844–1900

Everyone has talent at twenty-five. The difficulty is to have it at fifty.

Edward Degas, 1834–1917

The father of every good work is discontent, and its mother is diligence.

Lajos Kassak, 1887–1967

If you steal from one author, it's plagiarism; if you steal from many, it's research.

Wilson Mizner, 1876–1933

The oldest books are still only just out to those who have not read them.

Samuel Butler, 1835–1902

Doubt grows with knowledge.

Johann Wolfgang von Goethe, 1749–1834

Hell is full of musical amateurs: Music is the brandy of the damned.

George Bernard Shaw, 1856–1950

The limits of my language mean the limits of my world.

Ludwig Josef Johann Wittgenstein, 1889–1951

Rules and models destroy genius and art.

William Hazlitt, 1778–1830

A journalist is stimulated by a deadline: He writes worse when he has time.

Karl Kraus, 1874–1936

Language most shows a man; speak that I may see thee.

Ben Jonson, c. 1573–1637

Why not go out on a limb? Isn't that where the fruit is?

Frank Scully, 1892–1964

Books are good enough in their own way, but they are a mighty bloodless substitute for life.

Robert Louis Stevenson, 1850–1894

Of the truly creative no one is ever master; it must be left to go its own way.

Johann Wolfgang von Goethe, 1749–1834

Every man is a borrower and a mimic; life is theatrical and literature a quotation.

Ralph Waldo Emerson, 1803–1882

Individuality of expression is the beginning and the end of all art.

Johann Wolfgang von Goethe, 1749–1834

All beauty comes from beautiful blood and a beautiful brain.

Walter Whitman, 1819–1892

Read over your compositions, and when you meet a passage which you think is particularly fine, strike it out.

Dr. Samuel Johnson, 1709–1784

Great geniuses have the shortest biographies: Their cousins can tell you nothing about them.

Ralph Waldo Emerson, 1803–1882

Our principal writers have nearly all been fortunate in escaping regular education.

Hugh MacDiarmid [Christopher Murray Grieve], 1892–1978

Censorship, like charity, should begin at home; but unlike charity, it should end there.

Clare Booth Luce, 1903–1987

The formula "two and two make five" is not without its attractions.

Fedor Dostoevsky, 1821–1881

I would as soon write free verse as play tennis with the net down.

Robert Frost, 1874–1963

A good writer is basically a story-teller, not a scholar or a redeemer of mankind.

Isaac Bashevis Singer, 1904–1991

As to the adjective: When in doubt, strike it out.

Mark Twain [Samuel Langhorne Clemens], 1835–1910

The man who does not read good books has no advantage over the man who can't read them.

Mark Twain [Samuel Langhorne Clemens], 1835–1910

The original writer is not one who imitates nobody, but one whom nobody can imitate.

François Rene de Chateaubriand, 1768–1848

Art is either plagiarism or revolution.

Paul Gauguin, 1848–1903

Connoisseurs think the art is already done.

John Constable, 1776–1857

If you're never scared or embarrassed or hurt, it means you never take any chances.

Julia Sorel [Rosalyn Drexler], 1926–

When we see a natural style we are quite amazed and delighted, because we expected to see an author and find a man.

Blaise Pascal, 1623–1662

If you educate a man you educate a person, but if you educate a woman you educate a family.

Ruby Manikan

Immature poets imitate; mature poets steal.

Thomas Stearns Eliot, 1888–1965

The nicest thing about quotes is that they give us a nodding acquaintance with the originator which is often socially impressive.

Kenneth Williams, 1926–1988

Ignorance is the mother of admiration.

George Chapman, c. 1559–1634

Criticism is easy, art is difficult.

Phillipe Destouches, 1680–1754

A good spectator also creates.

Swiss proverb

Some books seem to have been written, not to teach us anything, but to let us know that the author has known something.

Johann Wolfgang von Goethe, 1749–1834

The difference between journalism and literature is that journalism is unreadable and literature is not read.

Oscar Wilde, 1854–1900

Let blockheads read what blockheads wrote.

Lord Philip Dormer Stanhope Chesterfield, 1694–1773

Keep to yourself the final touches of your art.

Baltasar Gracian, 1601–1658

In the case of good books, the point is not to see how many of them you can get through, but rather how many can get through to you.

Mortimer Jerome Adler, 1902–

If you can speak what you will never hear, if you can write what you will never read, you have done rare things.

Henry David Thoreau, 1817–1862

Whate'er is well conceived is clearly said, and the words to say it flow with ease.

Nicholas Boileau-Despreaux, 1636–1711

I couldn't wait for success . . . so I went ahead without it.

Jonathan Winters, 1925–

The most essential gift for a good writer is a built-in, shockproof crap detector. This is the writer's radar and all great writers have had it.

Ernest Hemingway, 1899–1961

We can say nothing but what hath been said. Our poets steal from Homer. . . . Our story-dressers do as much; he that comes last is commonly best.

Robert Burton, 1577–1640

Literature is mostly about having sex and not much about having children; life is the other way round.

David Lodge, 1935–

An example of the monkey: The higher it climbs, the more you see of its behind.

Saint Bonaventure, 1217–1274

Words and sentences are subjects of revision; paragraphs and whole compositions are subjects of prevision.

Barrett Wendell, 1855–1921

Talent is commonly developed at the expense of character.

Ralph Waldo Emerson, 1803–1882

One becomes a critic when one cannot be an artist, just as a man becomes a stool pigeon when he cannot be a soldier.

Gustave Flaubert, 1821–1880

There is nothing more dreadful than imagination without taste.

Johann Wolfgang von Goethe, 1749–1834

Autobiography is an unrivaled vehicle for telling the truth about other people.

Philip Guedalla, 1889–1944

A great deal of talent is lost to the world for want of a little courage.

Sydney Smith, 1771–1845

To me the charm of an encyclopedia is that it knows—and I needn't.

Francis Yeats-Brown, 1886–1944

The reason why so few good books are written is that so few people who can write know anything.

Walter Bagehot, 1826–1877

I've put my genius into my life; I've only put my talent into my works.

Oscar Wilde, 1854–1900

There is no such thing as a moral or an immoral book. Books are well written, or badly written.

Oscar Wilde, 1854–1900

True genius walks along a line, and, perhaps, our greatest pleasure is in seeing it so often near falling, without being ever actually down.

Oliver Goldsmith, 1728–1774

Well-timed silence hath more eloquence than speech.

Martin Farquhar Tupper, 1810–1889

He who does not know foreign languages does not know anything about his own.

Johann Wolfgang von Goethe, 1749–1834

Abstract Expressionism was invented by New York drunks.

Joni Mitchell, 1943–

They lard their lean books with the fat of others' works.

Robert Burton, 1577–1640

Weak men are the worse for the good sense they read in books because it furnisheth them only with more matter to mistake.

George Savile, Marquess de Halifax, 1633–1695

A poem is never finished, only abandoned.

Paul Valéry, 1871–1945

A book is a mirror: If an ass peers into it, you can't expect an apostle to look out.

Georg Christoph Lichtenberg, 1742–1799

What's past is prologue.

William Shakespeare, 1564–1616

As for style of writing, if one has anything to say, it drops from him simply and directly, as a stone falls to the ground.

Henry David Thoreau, 1817–1862

"Classic": a book which people praise and don't read.

Mark Twain [Samuel Langhorne Clemens], 1835–1910

Autobiography is a preemptive strike against biographers.

Barbara G. Harrison, 1941–

The true use of speech is not so much to express our wants as to conceal them.

Oliver Goldsmith, 1728–1774

To do easily what is difficult for others is the mark of talent. To do what is impossible for talent is the mark of genius.

Henri Frédéric Amiel, 1821–1881

The act of writing is the act of discovering what you believe.

David Hare, 1947–

It takes taste to account for taste.

Spanish proverb

Music begins to atrophy when it departs too far from the dance . . . poetry begins to atrophy when it gets too far from music.

Ezra Pound, 1885–1972

Opportunities are usually disguised as hard work, so most people don't recognize them.

Ann Landers [Esther P. Lederer], 1918–

What we anticipate seldom occurs; what we least expected generally happens.

Benjamin Disraeli, Earl of Beaconsfield, 1804–1881

A book is a success when people who haven't read it pretend they have.

Los Angeles Times Syndicate

It is with words as with sunbeams. The more they are condensed, the deeper they burn.

Robert Southey, 1774–1843

Of all cold words of tongue or pen, the worst are these: "I knew him when—"

Arthur Guiterman, 1871–1943

Classical music is the kind we keep thinking will turn into a tune.

Frank McKinney "Kin" Hubbard, 1868–1930

It is easier to understand a nation by listening to its music than by learning its language.

Anonymous

How vain it is to sit down to write when you have not stood up to live.

Henry David Thoreau, 1817–1862

No poems can please for long or live that are written by water-drinkers.

Horace [Quintus Horatius Flaccus], 65–8 B.C.

Show me a great actor and I'll show you a lousy husband. Show me a great actress, and you've seen the devil.

W. C. Fields, 1880–1946

The few bad poems which occasionally are created during abstinence are of no great interest.

Wilhelm Reich, 1897–1959

No place affords a more striking conviction of the vanity of human hopes than a public library.

Dr. Samuel Johnson, 1709–1784

Music is the brandy of the damned.

George Bernard Shaw, 1856-1950

I have made this letter longer than usual, because I lack the time to make it short.

Blaise Pascal, 1623–1662

Most people have to talk so they won't hear.

May Sarton, 1912–1995

Few men make themselves masters of the things they write or speak.

John Selden, 1584–1654

Adversity has the effect of eliciting talents which, in prosperous circumstances, would have lain dormant.

Horace [Quintus Horatius Flaccus], 65–8 B.C.

He who pretends to be either painter or engraver without being a master of drawing is an impostor.

William Blake, 1757–1827

Journalists write because they have nothing to say, and have something to say because they write.

Karl Kraus, 1874–1936

Law school is the opposite of sex. Even when it's good it's lousy.

Anonymous

One man's wage rise is another man's price increase.

Harold Wilson, Baron of Rievaulx, 1916–1995

Make voyages!—Attempt them! There's nothing else.

Tennessee Williams [Thomas Lanier], 1911–1983

One can present people with opportunities. One cannot make them
equal to them.

Rosamond Lehmann, 1901–1990

Take care how thou offendest men raised from low condition.

Thomas Fuller, 1654–1734

The world is divided into two classes—invalids and nurses.

James McNeill Whistler, 1834–1903

Art hath an enemy called ignorance.

Ben Jonson, c. 1573–1637

Be wise today; 'tis madness to defer.

Edward Young, 1683–1765

Expansion means complexity, and complexity decay.

Cyril Northcote Parkinson, 1909–1993

While we stop to think, we often miss our opportunity.

Publilius Syrus, first century B.C.

The great artists of the world are never Puritans, and seldom even ordinarily respectable.

Henry Louis Mencken, 1880–1956

Equality of opportunity means equal opportunity to be unequal.

Fiona Mcleod [William Sharp], 1855–1905

Bad artists always admire each other's work.

Oscar Wilde, 1854–1900

A throw of the dice will never abolish chance.

Stéphane Mallarmé, 1842–1898

Modern art is what happens when painters stop looking at girls and persuade themselves that they have a better idea.

John Anthony Ciardi, 1916–1986

Grab a chance and you won't be sorry for a might have been.

Arthur Mitchell Ransome, 1884–1967

Misspending a man's time is a kind of self-homicide.

George Savile, Marquess de Halifax, 1633–1695

A woman is fascinated not by art but by the noise made by those in the field.

Anton Pavlovich Chekhov, 1860–1904

12

History and Government

The century is advanced, but every individual begins afresh.

Johann Wolfgang von Goethe, 1749–1834

The handwriting on the wall may be a forgery.

Ralph Hodgson, 1871–1962

The best of prophets of the future is the past.

George Noel Gordon, Lord Byron, 1788–1824

Every beginning is a consequence—every beginning ends something.

Paul Valéry, 1871–1945

Nearly all men can stand adversity, but if you want to test a man's character, give him power.

Abraham Lincoln, 1809–1865

It is horrible to see everything that one detested in the past coming back wearing the colors of the future.

Jean Rostand, 1894–1977

Perhaps in time the so-called Dark Ages will be thought of as including our own.

Georg Christoph Lichtenberg, 1742–1799

Throughout history the world has been laid waste to ensure the triumph of conceptions that are now as dead as the men that died for them.

Henry de Montherlant, 1896–1972

Freedom of the press is guaranteed only to those who own one.

Abbott Joseph Liebling, 1904–1963

In war, there are no unwounded soldiers.

José Narosky

Those who cannot remember the past are condemned to repeat it.

George Santayana, 1863–1952

Let him not boast who puts his armor on as he who puts it off, the battle done.

Henry Wadsworth Longfellow, 1807–1882

The world is ruled by force, not by opinion; but opinion uses force.

Blaise Pascal, 1623–1662

War hath no fury like a non-combatant.

Charles Edward Montague, 1867–1928

The worst form of tyranny the world has ever known: the tyranny of the weak over the strong. It is the only tyranny that lasts.

Oscar Wilde, 1854–1900

Fortune soon tires of carrying anyone long on her shoulders.

Baltasar Gracian, 1601–1658

Unanimity is almost always an indication of servitude.

Charles de Remusat, 1797–1875

The point to remember is that what the government gives it must first take away.

John Strider Coleman, 1897–1958

An army of sheep led by a lion would defeat an army of lions led by a sheep.

Arab proverb

The oldest, wisest politician grows not more human so, but is merely a gray wharf rat at last.

Henry David Thoreau, 1817–1862

Any class is all right if it will only let others be so.

Samuel Butler, 1835–1902

A military operation involves deception. Even though you are competent, appear to be incompetent. Though effective, appear to be ineffective.

Sun-tzu, fourth century B.C.

Power does not corrupt men; fools, however, if they get into a position of power, corrupt power.

George Bernard Shaw, 1856–1950

A court is an assembly of noble and distinguished beggars.

Charles Maurice, Prince de Talleyrand-Périgord, 1754–1838

Agree, for the law is costly.

Sir William Camden, 1551–1623

No government can be long secure without a formidable opposition.

Benjamin Disraeli, Earl of Beaconsfield, 1804–1881

The law, in its majestic equality, forbids the rich as well as the poor to sleep under bridges, to beg in the streets, and to steal bread.

Anatole France [Jacques Anatole François Thibault], 1844–1924

There is a holy mistaken zeal in politics as well as in religion. By persuading others, we convince ourselves.

"The Letters of Junius," 1769–1771

Politicians neither love nor hate. Interest, not sentiment, directs them.

Lord Philip Dormer Stanhope Chesterfield, 1694–1774

Democracy passes into despotism.

Plato, c. 428–348 B.C.

The world of politics is always twenty years behind the world of thought.

John Jay Chapman, 1862–1933

Whenever a man has cast a longing eye on offices, a rottenness begins in his conduct.

Thomas Jefferson, 1743–1826

Laws are like cobwebs, which may catch small flies, but let wasps and hornets break through.

Jonathan Swift, 1667–1745

A liberal is a man who will give away everything he doesn't own.

Frank Dane

When smashing monuments, save the pedestals—they always come in handy.

Stanislaw Jerzy Lec 1909–1966

He that would govern others, first should be the master of himself.

Philip Massinger, 1583–1640

Equality of opportunity is an equal opportunity to prove unequal talents.

Lord Herbert Louis Samuel, 1870–1916

The art of taxation consists in so plucking the goose as to get the most feathers with the least hissing.

Ascribed to Jean Baptist Colbert, 1619–1683

When there is an income tax, the just will pay more and the unjust less.

Plato, c. 428–348 B.C.

Victorious warriors win first and then go to war, while defeated warriors go to war first and then seek to win.

Sun-tzu, fourth century B.C.

All rising to great place is by a winding stair.

Sir Francis Bacon, 1561–1626

Assassination is the extreme form of censorship.

George Bernard Shaw, 1856–1950

There is a demand today for men who can make wrong appear right.

Terence [Publius Terentius Afer], c. 190–159 B.C.

Nothing doth more hurt in a state than that cunning men pass for wise.

Sir Francis Bacon, 1561–1626

To get others to come into our ways of thinking, we must go over to theirs; and it is necessary to follow, in order to lead.

William Hazlitt, 1778–1830

Democracy becomes a government of bullies tempered by editors.

Ralph Waldo Emerson, 1803–1882

When you have robbed a man of everything, he is no longer in your power. He is free again.

Alexander Isayevich Solzhenitsyn, 1918–

When there is no middle class, and the poor greatly exceed in number, troubles arise, and the state soon comes to an end.

Aristotle, 384–322 B.C.

Never exceed your rights, and they will soon become unlimited.

Jean Jacques Rousseau, 1712–1778

Treaties are like roses and young girls—they last while they last.

Charles de Gaulle, 1890–1970

For those who govern, the first thing required is indifference to newspapers.

Louis Adolphe Thiers, 1797–1877

Nobody outside of a baby carriage or a judge's chamber believes in an unprejudiced point of view.

Lillian Hellman, 1905–1984

Democracy substitutes election by the incompetent many for appointment by the corrupt few.

George Bernard Shaw, 1856–1950

None can love freedom heartily, but good men; the rest love not freedom, but license.

John Milton, 1608–1674

Let the people think they govern, and they will be governed.

William Penn, 1644–1718

Equality is the result of human organization. We are not born equal.

Hannah Arendt, 1906–1975

Be extremely subtle, to the point of formlessness. Be extremely mysterious, to the point of soundlessness. Thereby you can be the director of the opponent's fate.

Sun-tzu, fourth century B.C.

We hang the petty thieves and appoint the great ones to public office.

Aesop, c. 550 B.C.

All animals are equal, but some animals are more equal than others.

George Orwell [Eric Blair], 1903–1950

13

Stuff to Think About

We probably wouldn't worry about what people think of us if we could know how seldom they do.

Olin Miller

What people say behind your back is your standing in the community.

Edgar Watson Howe, 1853–1937

The thorns which I have reaped are of the tree I planted.

George Noel Gordon, Lord Byron, 1788–1824

Advice is what we ask for when we already know the answer but wish we didn't.

Erica Jong, 1942–

One of the oldest human needs is having someone to wonder where you are when you don't come home at night.

Margaret Mead, 1901–1978

A guest sees more in an hour than the host in a year.

Polish proverb

There is no little enemy.

Benjamin Franklin, 1706–1790

It is easy—terribly easy—to shake a man's faith in himself. To take advantage of that, to break a man's spirit is devil's work.

George Bernard Shaw, 1856–1950

The more help a person has in his garden, the less it belongs to him.

William H. Davies, 1871–1940

The creditor hath a better memory than the debtor.

James Howell, c. 1594–1666

Ridicule often checks what is absurd, and fully as often smothers that which is noble.

Sir Walter Scott, 1771–1832

No man is angry that feels not himself hurt.

Sir Francis Bacon, 1561–1626

Tact is the knack of making a point without making an enemy.

Sir Isaac Newton, 1642–1727

Luck affects everything. Let your hook always be cast; in the stream where you least expect it there will be a fish.

Ovid [Publius Ovidius Naso], 43 B.C.–18 A.D.

I don't want to see the uncut version of anything.

Jean Kerr, 1923–

Advice is seldom welcome; and those who want it the most always like it the least.

Lord Philip Dormer Stanhope Chesterfield, 1694–1773

When a stupid man is doing something he is ashamed of, he always declares that it is his duty.

George Bernard Shaw, 1856–1950

Tact is the art of convincing people that they know more than you do.

Raymond Mortimer, 1895–1980

A yawn is a silent shout.

Gilbert Keith Chesterton, 1874–1936

Saint, *n.* A dead sinner revised and edited.

Ambrose Bierce, 1842–c. 1914

Analysis kills spontaneity. The grain once ground into flour springs and germinates no more.

Henri Frédéric Amiel, 1821–1881

Fortune favors the bold but abandons the timid.

Latin proverb

To be agreeable in society, you must consent to be taught many things which you already know.

Charles Maurice, Prince de Talleyrand-Périgord, 1754–1838

Skepticism is the chastity of the intellect, and it is shameful to surrender it too soon or to the first comer.

George Santayana, 1863–1952

Never explain. Your friends do not need it and your enemies will not believe it anyway.

Elbert Hubbard, 1856–1915

Charm is the quality in others that makes us more satisfied with ourselves.

Henri Frédéric Amiel, 1821–1881

A synonym is a word you use when you can't spell the other one.

Baltasar Gracian, 1601–1658

Wit makes its own welcome, and levels all distinctions.

Ralph Waldo Emerson, 1803–1882

If the camel once gets his nose in a tent, his body will soon follow.

Saudi Arabian proverb

The manner in which it is given is worth more than the gift.

Pierre Corneille, 1606–1684

Nothing is so silly as the expression of a man who is being complimented.

André Gide, 1869–1951

Gratitude is a useless word. You will find it in a dictionary but not in life.

François, Duc de La Rochefoucauld, 1613–1680

They say best men are molded out of faults, and, for the most, become much more the better for being a little bad.

William Shakespeare, 1564–1616

Too great haste in paying off an obligation is a kind of ingratitude.

François, Duc de La Rochefoucauld, 1613–1680

A professional is someone who can do his best work when he doesn't feel like it.

Alfred Alistair Cooke, 1908–

The joke loses everything when the joker laughs himself.

Johann Christoph Friedrich von Schiller, 1775–1854

Solemnity is the shield of idiots.

> *Charles Louis de Secondat, Baron de Montesquieu, 1689–1750*

The marvelous thing about a joke with a double meaning is that it can only mean one thing.

> *Ronnie Barker, 1929–*

Nothing lowers the level of conversation more than raising the voice.

> *Stanley Horowitz, 1925*

All that we do is done with an eye to something else.

> *Aristotle, 384–322 B.C.*

If you want to be witty, work on your character and say what you think on every occasion.

> *Marie-Henri Beyle Stendhal, 1783–1843*

Beware the flatterer: He feeds you with an empty spoon.

> *Cosino De Gregrio*

Any man's death diminishes me, because I am involved in mankind; and therefore never send to know for whom the bell tolls; it tolls for thee.

John Donne, 1572–1631

Your worst humiliation is only someone else's momentary entertainment.

Karen Crockett

The silliest woman can manage a clever man; but it needs a very clever woman to manage a fool!

Rudyard Kipling, 1865–1936

A fair request should be followed by the deed in silence.

Dante Alighieri, 1265–1321

Being defeated is often a temporary condition. Giving up is what makes it permanent.

Marlene vos Savant, 1946–

The well of true wit is truth itself.

George Meredith, 1828–1909

Wit and wisdom are born with a man.

John Selden, 1584–1654

Education is learning what you didn't even know you didn't know.

Daniel J. Boorstin, 1914–

Our repugnance to death increases in proportion to our consciousness of having lived in vain.

William Hazlitt, 1778–1830

To escape criticism—do nothing, say nothing, be nothing.

Elbert Hubbard, 1856–1915

Without education, we are in a horrible and deadly danger of taking educated people seriously.

Gilbert Keith Chesterton, 1874–1936

The vanity of teaching doth oft tempt a man to forget that he is a blockhead.

George Savile, Marquess de Halifax, 1633–1695

I tell you the past is a bucket of ashes.

Carl Sandburg, 1878–1967

Wit has truth in it; wisecracking is simply calisthenics with words.

Dorothy Parker, 1893–1967

One sword keeps another in the sheath.

George Herbert, 1593–1633

The greatest fault of a penetrating wit is to go beyond the mark.

François, Duc de La Rochefoucauld, 1613–1680

In every work of genius, we recognize our own rejected thoughts; they come back to us with a certain alienated majesty.

Ralph Waldo Emerson, 1803–1882

Wit is far more often a shield than a lance.

Anonymous

Better never than late.

George Bernard Shaw, 1856–1950

The ultimate result of shielding men from the effects of folly is to fill the world with fools.

Herbert Spencer, 1820–1903

First you take a drink, then the drink takes a drink, then the drink takes you.

Francis Scott Key Fitzgerald, 1896–1940

Fear leads you directly into the path of that which you fear.

Anonymous

If you are seeking creative ideas, go out walking. Angels whisper to a man when he goes for a walk.

Raymond Inmon

Wisdom comes alone through suffering.

Aeschylus, 525–456 B.C.

Sources

Cindy Adams: Joey Adams, *Cindi and I,* 1957 (ch. 2, p. 67).

Franklin P. Adams: *Ballade of Schopenhauer's Philosophy,* (ch. 1, p. 6).

Henry Brooks Adams: *The Education of Henry Adams,* 1907, ch. 31
    (chs. 1, p. 21; 4, p. 101).

Joseph Addison: *Cato,* 1713, act 1, scene 4 (ch. 7, p. 178).

Alfred Adler: *Sam Walton,* 1992, p. 5 (ch. 1, p. 62).

Renata Adler: "What's So Funny?" *New York Times,* July 7, 1968 (ch. 9, p. 202).

Aeschylus:
    Agamemnon, c. 458 B.C (ch. 6, p. 144).
    Prometheus Bound, c. 478 B.C. (ch. 13, p. 289).

Aesop: "The Eagle and the Arrow," *The Fables,* c. 550 B.C. (ch. 10, p. 229).

Bronson Alcott:
    "Discourse," *Table Talk,* 1877 (ch. 6, p. 156).
    Table Talk, 1868 (ch. 11, p. 233).

Ali ibn-Abi-Talib: *A Hundred Sayings,* 1993 (ch. 1, p. 63).

Dante Alighieri:
    The Divine Comedy, Inferno, c. 1310–1321, canto 1, 1. 32 (ch. 1, "This miserable
        state . . . , " p. 9), canto 24, l. 77 (chs. 4, p. 106; 13, p. 286).
    Paradisio, canto 1, l. 34 (ch. 1, "A great flame . . . ," p. 41).

Henri Frédéric Amiel:
    Journal Intime, 1882–1884, entry no. 22 (ch. 6, p. 146).
    Journal Intime, entry for December 17, 1856 (ch. 11, p. 260).
    Journal Intime, entry for November 7, 1878 (ch. 13, "Analysis kills . . , " p. 282).
    Journal, 1882–1884, (ch. 13, "Charm is . . , " p. 283).

Maya Angelou: *I Know Why the Caged Bird Sings,* 1969, ch. 17 (ch. 9, p. 200).

Jean Anouilh: *Becket,* 1963, (ch. 10, p. 215).

Antisthenes: quoted in Diogenes Laertius, *Lives of the Philosophers,* (ch. 11, p. 237).

Minna Antrim: *Naked Truth and Veiled Allusions,* 1901, p. 99 1901 (ch. 1, p. 43).

Hannah Arendt: *Origins of Totalitarianism,* 1951 (ch. 12, p. 277).

Aristophanes: *The Birds,* c. 415 B.C. (ch. 3, p. 91).

Aristotle:
    Nicomachean Ethics, c. 350 B.C.E., 3.3 (ch. 13, p. 285) and 3.4 (ch. 11, "What it lies
        . . , " p. 240).
    Politics, c. 350 B.C.E. (chs. 1, p. 40; 9, p. 196; 10, p. 219; 12, p. 275).
    quoted in Diogenes Laertius, *Lives of the Philosophers,* book 5, sect. 19
        (ch. 11, "Educated men . . , " p. 237).

Henri Arnold: quoted in Reader's Digest, *Quotable Quotes,* 1997 (ch. 9, p. 196).

Matthew Arnold: "Self-Dependence," *Empedocles on Etna, and Other Poems,* 1852, 1l.
    31–32 (ch. 1, p. 53).

Isaac Asimov: *Reader's Digest,* October 1977 (ch. 10, p. 214).

W. H. Auden: attributed (ch. 11, p. 214).

Saint Augustine: *Confessions,* book 8, ch. 7, pp. 397–398 (ch. 8, p. 187).

Marcus Aurelius: *Meditations,* c. 100–200, 12.4 (ch. 6, p. 135, p. 148).

Sir Francis Bacon:
>From *Essays,* 1625, "Of Fortune" (ch. 2, p. 68).
>
>"Of Ceremonies and Respects" (ch. 6, p. 136).
>
>"Of Marriage and Single Life" (ch. 9, "He that hath . . . , " p. 196).
>
>"Of Parents and Children" (ch. 9, "The joys of parents . . . ," p. 199).
>
>"Of Studies" (ch. 11, p. 238).
>
>"Of Great Place" (ch. 12, "All rising . . . ," p. 274).
>
>"Of Cunning" (ch. 12, "Nothing doth . . . ," p. 275).
>
>"Of Anger" (ch. 13, p. 280).

Walter Bagehot:
>*Literary Studies,* 1879 (ch. 1, p. 36).
>
>*Hartley Coleridge,* 1852, reprinted in *Literary Studies,* 1878 (ch. 4, p. 108).
>
>*Biographical Studies,* 1972 (ch. 7, p. 163).
>
>"Shakespeare," *Literary Studies,* 1879 (ch. 11, p. 257).

James Baldwin:
>"The Precarious Vogue of Ingmar Bergman," first published in *Esquire,* April 1960, reprinted in *Nobody Knows My Name,* 1961 (ch. 9, p. 193).
>
>"The Black Boy Looks at the White Boy," *Nobody Knows My Name* (ch. 11, p. 240).

Honoré de Balzac:
>"Scenes de la vie Parisienne," *La Maison Nucingen,* vol. 3, 1838 (ch. 1, p. 58).
>
>*La muse du département,* 1843 (chs. 6, p. 154; 10, p. 216).

Ronnie Barker: "Daddie's Sauce," *Sauce,* 1977 (ch. 13, p. 285).

Sir Cecil Walter Hardy Beaton: Stated by Cecil Beaton of Evelyn Waugh (ch. 10, p. 228).

Simone de Beauvoir: *All Men Are Mortal,* 1955 (ch. 2, p. 73).

Henry Ward Beecher:
>*Proverbs from Plymouth Pulpit,* 1887 (chs. 1, p. 19; 7, p. 168; and 10 ["Never forget . . . ,"] p. 219).
>
>>quoted by Peter Potter, *All About Success,* 1988 (ch. 10, "In things pertaining . . . ," p. 219).

Sir Max Beerbolm: quoted in S. N. Behrman, *Conversations with Max,* 1960, but also attributed to Jean Girandoux and W. Somerset Maugham (ch. 1, p. 47).

Bernard Berenson: *Notebook,* 1892 (ch. 5, p. 119).

George Bishop Berkeley:
>*Maxims Concerning Patriotism,* 1740 (ch. 3, "He who says . . . ," p. 81).
>
>*Siris,* 1744 (ch. 3, "Truth is . . . ," p. 81).

Louis Hector Berlioz: Said of Meyerbeer, "The luck of having talent was not enough; he also had a talent for luck" (ch. 11, p. 247).

Claude Bernard: *Introduction to the Study of Experimental Medicine,* 1865 (ch. 11, p. 235).

Princess Elizabeth Bibesco: *Haven,* 1951 (ch. 1, "Endurance . . . ," p. 7, and "To others . . . ," p. 10).

Ambrose Bierce:
    The Devil's Dictionary, 1881–1906, p. 86 (ch. 1, p. 50).
    p. 41 (ch. 2, p. 74 *or* p. 77).
    p. 37 (ch. 4, p. 103).
    p. 306 (chs. 7, p. 175; 13, p. 282).
    The Enlarged Devil's Dictionary, 1906, (ch. 10, p. 213).

Josh Billings (Henry Wheeler Shaw):
    Josh Billings: His Sayings, 1865, ch. 39 (ch. 1, "It is a very . . . ," p. 46).
    The Kicker (ch. 1, "Better make . . . ," p. 6).
    "Hooks and Eyes," *Everybody's Friend,* 1971, (ch. 8, p. 188).
    Reader's Digest, *Quotable Quotes,* 1997 (ch. 9, p. 210).
    On Ice, 1868, p. 138 (ch. 11, p. 239).

Bion: "Water and Land Animals," *Plutarch,* (ch. 1, p. 46).

William Blake:
    "Auguries of Innocence," *Poems from the Pickering Manuscript,* c. 1805, 1. 53 (ch. 3, p. 86).
    "There Is No Natural Religion" (ch. 6, p. 161).
    "The Marriage of Heaven and Hell," *Proverbs of Hell,* 1790–1793, 1. 3 (ch. 8, 187).

Nicholas Boileau-Despreaux: *L'art poétique,* 1674 (chs. 1, p. 55; 11, p. 255).

Saint Bonaventure: *Conferences on the Gospel of John,* (ch. 11, p. 256).

Daniel J. Boorstin: "A Case of Hypochondria," *Newsweek,* July 6, 1970 (ch. 13, p. 287).

James Boswell: *Life of Johnson,* 1791, footnote, March 30, 1778 (ch. 4, p. 96).

Elizabeth Dorothea Cole Bowen: *The House in Paris,* 1935 (ch. 10, p. 228).

F. H. Bradley: *Aphorisms,* 1930 (chs. 1, p. 28; 6, p. 141).

Wernher von Braun: Reader's Digest, *Quotable Quotes,* 1997 (ch. 9, p. 199).

John Bright: Attributed comment about Benjamin Disraeli (ch. 8, p. 182).

Anthelme Brillat-Savarin: *La physiologie du gout* (The physiology of taste), 1825 (ch. 1, p. 47).

Broadhurst: "To the Celebrated Beauties of the British Court," early eighteenth century (ch. 4, p. 115).

Baron Henry Peter Brougham: Speech, 1828, published in *The Present State of the Law,* February 7, 1828 (ch. 11, p. 238).

Heywood Broun: Quoted in James A. Michener, *Sports in America,* 1976 (ch. 1, p. 26).

Sir Thomas Browne: *Christian Morals,* 1716, (ch. 5, p. 125).

Robert Browning: "Bishop Blougram's Apology" (ch. 1, p. 13).
Apollo and the Fates, prologue (ch. 2, p. 72).

Edmund Burke: "Speech on American Taxation," 1774 (ch. 1, "It is the nature . . . ,"
p. 10).
"Letter to a Member of the National Assembly" (ch. 1, "You can never . . . ," p. 53).
"Letters on a Regicide Peace," letter 1 (ch. 2, p. 67).
"Reflections on the Revolution in France" (ch. 10, p. 226).
"Speech on Conciliation with the American Colonies," March 22, 1775
(ch. 10, p. 227).

Robert Burton: "Anatomy of Melancholy," *Democritus to the Reader,* 1621,
(chs. 4, p. 106; 9 p. 207; and 11 ["We can say nothing . . . ," p. 255 and
"They lard . . . ," p. 258]).

Roger de Bussy-Rabutin: "Maximes d'amours," *Histoire amoureuse des Gaules,*
(ch. 1, p. 39).

Samuel Butler (1612–1680):
Prose Observations, 1660–1680 (chs. 1 ["There are more . . . ," p. 11 and "We grow
weary . . . ," p. 52] and 2 ["The first undertakers . . . ," p. 77]
Hudribas, pt. 2, ch. 2, 107 (chs. 2 ["Whatsoe'er . . . ," p. 70] and 4, p. 111).

Samuel Butler (1835–1902):
Note-Books, 1912, (ch. 1, "Man is the only . . . ." p. 45).
Note-Books, 1912, ch. 1 (ch. 8 ["All progress . . . ," p. 189 and
"Life is the art . . . ," p. 189]).
Note-Books, 1951, ch. 14 (ch. 4, "A definition . . . ," p. 110), p. 250 (ch. 4,
"Conscience is . . . ," p. 99), p. 221 (ch. 6, "Opinions have . . . ," p. 144),
p. 266 (ch. 11); "Speech at the Somerville Club," February 27, 1895
(ch. 1, "Life is like . . . ," p. 56).

Robert Byrne: *1,911 Best Things Anybody Ever Said,* 1988 (ch. 7, p. 164).

George Noel Gordon, Lord Byron:
Childe Harold's Pilgrimage, 1809–1817, canto 3, stanza 112 (ch. 9, p. 209), stanza 10
(ch. 13, p. 279).
Don Juan, 1821, ch. 1, l. line 179 (ch. 1, p. 21) and ch. 1, 1. line 179 (ch. 7, p. 165).
Journal, January 28, 1821 (ch. 12, p. 268).

Sir William Camden: *Remains,* 1605, (ch. 12, p. 272).

Albert Camus:
The Fall, 1956 (chs. 1, p. 25; 4, p. 95).
The Plague, 1947 (ch. 8, p. 187).

Sandra Carey: Reader's Digest, *Quotable Quotes,* 1997 (ch. 9, p. 191).

Andrew Carnegie:
> *Triumphant Democracy,* 1886 (ch. 9, p. 198).
> "Wealth," *North American Review,* June 1889 (ch. 10, p. 222).

George Washington Carver: Reader's Digest, *Quotable Quotes,* 1997 (ch. 7, p. 167).

Galius Valerius Catullus:
> *Carmina,* 1st c. B.C.E., no. 73 (ch. 1, p. 56).
> *Carmina,* 1st c. B.C.E., no. 70 (ch. 7, p. 179).

Susannah Centlivre: *The Artifice,* 1722, (ch. 3, p. 85).

Miguel de Cervantes:
> *Don Quixote de la Mancha,* 1605, pt. I, bk. I, ch. 4, p. 25 (ch. 1, p. 14).
> pt. I, bk, III, ch. 6, p. 133 (ch. 7, p. 174).

Sebastien Roch Nicolas Chamfort: *Characters and Anecdotes,* 1771 (ch. 1, "We have
> three kinds . . . ," p. 62).
> *Maxims and pensées,* vol. 2, no. 522, 1796 (ch. 6, "People are governed . . . ,"
> p. 136).
> *Maxims and pensées,* 1805, 52 (ch. 3, p. 82).
> *Maxims and pensées,* 1805, 52 (ch. 1, "If we would please . . . ," p. 41).

Raymond Chandler: from his notes on the mystery novel, 1949 (ch. 11, p. 245).

George Chapman:
> *All Fools,* c. 1599, (ch. 9, p. 198).
> *The Widow's Tears,* 1612 (ch. 11, p. 253).

John Jay Chapman: John Jay Chapman to S. S. Drury, May 18, 1914 (ch. 10,
> p. 212).

Émile Auguste Chartier:
> *Le citoyen contre les pouvoirs,* 1925, (chs. 1, p. 2 and 6 ["To think . . . ," p. 135]).
> *Propos sur la religion,* no. 74, 1938 (ch. 6, "Nothing is more . . . ," p. 149).
> *Systeme des beaux-arts,* 1920 (ch. 1, "We prove . . . ," p. 34).

François Rene de Chateaubriand: *Le genie du christianisme,* 1802 (ch. 11, p. 252).

Malcolm de Chazal: Reader's Digest, *Quotable Quotes,* 1997 (ch. 8, p. 185).

Anton Pavlovich Chekhov:
> *Notebooks,* 1896 (ch. 6, p. 148).
> *The Selected Letters of Anton Chekhov,* (ch. 2, p. 68).

Lord Philip Dormer Stanhope Chesterfield:
> "Among Maxims Enclosed with a Letter to His Son," January 15, 1753 (ch. 4,
> "There are some . . . ," p. 111).
> Letters to his son, February 22, 1748 (ch. 4, "If you would . . . ," p. 96), April 30,
> 1750 (ch. 1, "People hate . . . ," p. 18), May 17, 1750 (ch. 5, "Modesty is . . . ,"
> p. 128), 1750 (ch. 4, "Every man . . . ," p. 109), November 24, 1749 (ch. 6, "Style
> is . . . ," p. 152), July 20, 1749 (ch. 5, "Idleness is . . . ," p. 131), 1750 (ch. 6,

"Knowledge may give . . . ," p. 155), November 1, 1750 (chs. 6 ["Pocket all . . . ," p. 157] and 11 ["Let blockheads . . . ," p. 254]), February 22, 1748 (ch. 6, "Wear your learning . . . ," p. 159), October 4, 1746 (ch. 6, "The knowledge of the world . . . , p. 160"), January 29, 1748 (ch. 13, "Advice is seldom . . . , p. 281"), *Letters,* 1748 (ch. 12, "Politicians neither . . . ," p. 272).

Gilbert Keith Chesterton:
 Heretics, 1905 (ch. 1 ["The people who . . . ," p. 36]).
 Orthodoxy, 1909, (ch. 10, "Do not free . . . ," p. 215).
 "The Real Dr. Johnson," *The Common Man,* 1950 (ch. 10, "A stiff apology . . . ," p. 212).

Sir Winston Spencer Churchill:
 Reader's Digest, December 1954 (ch. 1, "An appeaser . . . ," p. 26).
 "Alfonso XIII," *Great Contemporaries,* 1937 (ch. 1, "A fanatic is . . . ," p. 43).

Count Galeazzo Ciano:
 Diario, entry for September 9, 1942 (ch. 2, p. 69).
 President Kennedy reportedly made this same remark in the wake of the Bay of Pigs invasion in April 1961.

John Anthony Ciardi: *Saturday Review,* January 23, 1957 (ch. 9, p. 208), and (ch. 11, p. 266).

Frank A. Clark: *Reader's Digest, Quotable Quotes,* 1997 (chs. 9, p. 203; 11, p. 245).

Georges Clemenceau: "Conversation with Jean Martet, December 18, 1927," published in Clemenceau, *The Events of His Life as Told by Himself to His Former Secretary, Jean Martet,* 1930, ch. 11, p. 67 (ch. 10, p. 218).

Barnett Cocks: Attributed (ch. 11, p. 242).

Jean Cocteau: (ch. 1, p. 49); "Le rappel el ordre," *Le coquet l'arlequin,* 1926, reprinted in *Collected Works,* vol. 9, 1950 (ch. 4, p. 116); *Professional Secrets,* 1922 (ch. 8, p. 186).

Jean Baptist Colbert: Attributed (ch. 12, p. 274).

John Strider Coleman: Address to the Detroit Chamber of Commerce, (ch. 12, p. 270).

Samuel Taylor Coleridge:
 Biographia Literia, 1817 (ch. 5, p. 129), ch. 11 (ch. 1, "No man does . . . ," p. 15).
 Table Talk, (ch. 6, "No mind is . . . ," p. 140), August 20, 1833 (ch. 6, "Men of genius . . . ," p. 141).

John Churton Collins: *Aphorisms in the English Review,* 1914 (ch. 1 ["No one who . . . ," p. 20 "Never claim . . . ," p. 20 and "In prosperity . . . ," p. 61], ch. 4, ch. 5 ["Though pride . . . ," p. 123 and "If we escape . . . ," p. 127]), no. 40 (ch. 2, p. 71).

Charles Caleb Colton: *Lacon,* 1820–1822, vol. 1, no. 183 (ch. 4, p. 98), no. 324 (ch. 6, p. 158).

Dame Ivy Compton-Burnett: *Manservant and Maidservant,* 1947 (ch. 3, p. 86).
Comtesse Diane (Marie Josephine de Suin de Beausac): *Maximes de la vie,* 1908 (chs. 1,
    p. 19; 4, p. 101 and 6, p. 136).
Confucius: *Analects,* fifth century B.C. (ch. 6, p. 142).
William Congreve: *Love for Love,* 1695, act 3, scene 8 (ch. 10, p. 229), act 4, scene 14
    (ch. 7, p. 167).
Cyril Connolly:
    Enemies of Promise, 1938, ch. 16 (ch. 3, p. 82).
    Turnstile One (ed. V.S. Pritchett), 1948, (ch. 5, p. 128).
Joseph Conrad:
    "A Familiar Preface," *A Personal Record,* 1912 (ch. 7, p. 173).
    Under Western Eyes, 1911, pt. 2, ch. 4 (ch. 5, p. 130).
Alfred Alistair Cooke: Reader's Digest, *Quotable Quotes,* 1997 (ch. 13, p. 284).
Calvin Coolidge: "Veto of Salary Increase Bill," *Faith,* 1919, p. 173 (ch. 10, p. 216).
Pierre Corneille:
    Le menteur, 1644, act 1, scene 1 (ch. 13, p. 283).
    Rodogune, 1644, act 2, scene 4 (ch. 1, p. 35).
Georges Courteline: *La philosophie de Georges Courteline,* 1917 (chs. 5, p. 128; 9, p. 206).
Norman Cousins: *Saturday Review,* April 15, 1978 (ch. 9, p. 202).
Monta Crane: Reader's Digest, *Quotable Quotes,* 1997 (ch. 10, p. 223).
Karen Crockett: Reader's Digest, *Quotable Quotes,* 1997 (ch. 13, p. 286).
Justice Sir Charles Darling: *Scintillae Juris,* 1889 (chs. 3, p. 88; 4, p. 110).
William H. Davies: Reader's Digest, *Quotable Quotes,* 1997 (ch. 13, p. 280).
Edward de Bono: *Observer,* June 12, 1977 (ch. 1, p. 31).
Marie de Vichy-Chamrond, Marquise du Deffand:
    Letter to d'Alembert, July 7, 1763 (ch. 1, p. 42).
    Letters to Voltaire, 1759–1775 (ch. 7, p. 163).
Daniel Defoe: *An Appeal to Honor and Justice, Tho' it be of His Worst Enemies,* 1715
    (ch. 11, p. 235).
Edgar Degas: Quoted in R. H. Ives Gammell, *The Shop-Talk of Edgar Degas,* 1961 (ch.
    11, p. 248).
Charles de Gaulle:
    Attributed (ch. 1, p. 2).
    quoted in Robert W. Kent, *Money Talks,* 1985 (ch. 6, p. 159).
    Speech at Elysées Palace, July 2, 1963 (ch. 12, p. 276).
Cosino De Gregrio: Reader's Digest, *Quotable Quotes,* 1997 (ch. 13, p. 285).
Henry de Montherlant: *Explicit Mysterium,* 1931 (ch. 2, p. 74).
Duchess Diane de Poitiers: *A Book of Days,* 1910 (ch. 7, p. 175).
Vittorio de Sica: *Observer,* 1961 (ch. 1, p. 43).

Marlene Dietrich: "Forgiveness," *Marlene Dietrich's ABC,* 1962 (ch. 7, p. 170).

Demosthenes: *Third Olynthiac,* 349 B.C.E., sect. 19 (ch. 3, p. 91).

Chauncey Depew: After-dinner Speech, (ch. 6, p. 150).

Antoinette du Ligier de la Garde Deshoulières: *Réflexions diverses,* (ch. 6, p. 146).

Phillipe Destouches: *L'obstacle imprévu,* 1717, act 1, scene 6 (ch. 1, p. 30); *Le glorieux,* 1732, act 2, scene 5 (ch. 11, p. 253).

Emily Dickinson: *Poems by Emily Dickinson,* 2nd series, 1891 (ch. 10, p. 215).

Denis Diderot:
    Essai sur la mérite de la vertu, 1745, (ch. 5, "From fanaticism . . . ," p. 119).
    "Rameau's Nephew," in *Rameau's Nephew,* written 1762, published 1821, reprinted in *Selected Writings,* 1966 (ch. 5, "Virtue is praised . . . ," p. 126).

Benjamin Disraeli:
    Coningsby, 1844, book 2, ch. 1 (ch. 12, p. 272), book 3, ch. 6 (ch. 1, "Almost everything . . . ," p. 56 and "Youth is a . . . ," p. 52).
    Endymion, 1880, book 2, ch. 4 (ch. 11, "What we anticipate . . . ," p. 260).
    Lothair, 1870, ch. 35 (ch. 11, "You know who . . . ," p. 244).
    The Infernal Marriage, 1834 (ch. 1, "Next to knowing . . . ," p. 33).

John Donne:
    Devotions, 1623, no. 17 (ch. 13, p. 286).
    Holy Sonnets, before 1615, no. 9 (ch. 9, p. 199).
    "The Anagram," *Elegies,* no. 2 (ch. 7, p. 177).
    "The Triple Fool," stanza 2 (ch. 6, p. 138).

Fedor Dostoevsky:
    Notes from the Underground, 1864 (ch. 11, p. 251).
    The Brothers Karamazov, 1879–1880, book 8, ch. 3 (ch. 5, p. 132), book 12, ch. 5 (ch. 9, p. 201).

Arthur Conan Doyle:
    The Sign of Four, 1890, ch. 6 (ch. 3, p. 86).
    The Valley of Fear, 1915 (ch. 6, p. 151).

Peter Drucker: Quoted in Robert W. Kent, *Money Talks,* 1985 (ch. 11, p. 233).

John Dryden: *Absalom and Achitophel,* 1681, pt. 1 (chs. 1, p. 41; 5, p. 126).

Guillaume de Salluste Du Bartas: *Divine Weeks and Works,* 1578, Second Week, Fourth Day, book 2 (ch. 1, p. 23).

Alexandre Dumas, fils: *L'esprit d'Alexandre Dumas* (ed., Leon Treich), 1927, (ch. 7, p. 169).

Finley Peter Dunne: "Casual Observations," *Mr. Dooley's Opinions,* 1901, (ch. 1, "A fanatic . . . ," p. 8 and "Trust everyone . . . ," p. 38).

William J. Durant: Reader's Digest, *Quotable Quotes,* 1997 (ch. 9, 204).

Maria Edgeworth: *Almeria,* 1802 (ch. 5, p. 127).

Albert Einstein:
  Science and Religion, 1941 (ch. 8, p. 184).
  Scientific American, February 1976 (ch. 6, p. 138).
George Eliot:
  Adam Bede, 1859, ch. 17 (ch. 1, "It's but little good . . . ," p. 42), ch. 33 (ch. 1,
    "He was like a cock . . . ," p. 17).
  Impressions of Theophrastus Such, 1879 (ch. 4, p. 101).
  Romala, 1863 (ch. 9, p. 201).
  Silas Marner, 1861, ch. 18 (ch. 11, p. 239).
Thomas Stearns Eliot:
  Quoted in Robert Giroux, *The Education of an Editor,* 1982, p. 22 (ch. 11, "Most
    editors . . . ," p. 246).
  Philip Massinger, *The Sacred Wood,* 1920 (ch. 11, "Immature poets . . . ," p. 253).
Havelock Ellis: *On Life and Sex: Essays of Love and Virtue,* 1937, ch. 1 (ch. 10,
    p. 225).
Ralph Waldo Emerson:
  "Circles," *Essays,* 1st series, 1841 (ch. 2, "Nothing great . . . ," p. 76).
  Essays, 1st series, 1841 (ch. 9, "Life is a festival . . . ," p. 193).
  "Friendship," *Essays,* 1st series, 1841 (ch. 4, "Two may talk . . . ," p. 102).
  "Prudence," *Essays,* 1st series, 1841 (ch. 10, "In skating . . . ," p. 220).
  "Self Reliance," *Essays,* 1st series, 1841 (chs. 1 ["Whoso would . . . ," p. 8] and 13
    ["In every work of genius . . . ," p. 288]).
  "Culture," *The Conduct of Life,* 1860 (chs. 10 ["A great part . . . ," p. 228] and 6
    ["Solitude . . . ," p. 157]).
  "Experience," *Essays,* 2nd series, 1844 (ch. 5, "That which we call . . . ," p. 123).
  "Fate," *The Conduct of Life,* 1860 (chs. 10 ["The efforts which . . . ," p. 218] and
    9 ["Men are what . . . ," p. 198]).
  Journals, 1832 (ch. 9 "The chief mourner . . . ," p. 193).
  Journals, 1839 (ch. 6, "How we hate . . . ," p. 159).
  Journals, 1863 (ch. 4 ["You can take better care . . . ," p. 97] and ch. 7 ["Take
    egotism out . . . ," p. 171]).
  Journals, 1909–1914, entry written in 1847 (ch. 12, "Democracy becomes . . . ,"
    p. 275).
  Journals, vol. 3, p. 496 (ch. 6, "Between cultivated . . . ," p. 144).
  Journals, vol. 5 (ch. 10, "No great man . . . ," p. 224).
  Journals, vol. 6, p. 184 (ch. 8, "Are you not scared . . . ," p. 182).
  Nature, 1836/1849, sect. 4 (ch. 1, "All that Adam . . . ," p. 52).
  Plato or *The Philosopher, Representative Men,* 1850 (ch. 11, "Great geniuses . . . ,"
    p. 251).

Public and Private Education, (ch. 6, "Colleges hate . . . ," p. 149).

Reader's Digest, *Quotable Quotes,* 1997 (ch. 10, "All my best thoughts . . . ," p. 229).

"Success," *Society and Solitude,* (ch. 11, "Every man is . . . ," p. 250).

"The Comic," *Letters and Social Aims,* 1876 (chs. 1, p. 2 and 13, "Wit makes . . . ," p. 283) "The Scholar," *Lectures and Biographical Sketches,* 1883 (ch. 11, "Talent is commonly . . . ," p. 256).

"Worship," *The Conduct of Life,* 1860 (chs. 1 ["People seem not . . . ," p. 22] and 4 ["The louder he talked . . . ," p. 99]).

Reader's Digest, *Quotable Quotes,* 1997 (ch. 9, "You cannot . . . ," p. 205).

Epicurus: Quoted in Diogenes Laertius, *Lives of the Philosophers,* c. 3rd century B.C.E., book 10, sect. 125 (ch. 9, p. 195).

Euripides:

    Alexander, (ch. 1, "Waste not fresh . . . ," p. 48).

    Helen, 412 B.C. (ch. 3, p. 83).

    Phrixus, , fragment 830 (ch. 9, p. 192).

Barry Farber: Reader's Digest, *Quotable Quotes,* 1997 (ch. 9, p. 207).

Leslie Farber: *The Ways of the Will,* 1966 (ch. 5, p. 125).

François de Salignac de la Mothe Fénelon: "Letter to the Academy," 1760 (ch. 4, p. 100).

Francis Scott Key Fitzgerald:

    quoted in Jules Feiffer, *Ackroyd,* 1977, May 7, 1964 (ch. 13, p. 289).

    "The Note-Books (O)," *The Crack-Up,* 1945 (ch. 11, "If you're strong . . . ," p. 234).

R. I. Fitzhenry: *The Harper Book of Quotations,* 1993 (ch. 6, p. 153).

Gustave Flaubert:

    letter to Madame Louise Colet, August 12, 1846 (ch. 11, "One must not . . . ," p. 234).

    letter to Madame Louise Colet, October 22, 1846 (ch. 11, "One becomes a critic . . . ," p. 256).

    Madame Bovary, 1857 (ch. 7, p. 175).

Edward Morgan Forster: *Washington College Magazine,* Winter 1992, p. 11 (ch. 4, p. 109).

Anatole France:

    The Crime of Sylvestre Bonnard, December 24, 1849 (chs. 1 ["Those who have given . . . ," p. 60] and 5 ["People who have no . . . ," p. 131]).

    The Garden of Epicurus, 1894 (ch. 1, "I cling to . . . ," p. 54).

    The Red Lily, 1894, (ch. 12, p. 272).

    The Revolt of the Angels, 1914 (ch. 1, "The average man . . . ," p. 44).

Benjamin Franklin:

    Poor Richard's Almanack, June 1733 (ch. 1, "After three days . . . ," p. 45), February

1734 (ch. 1, "Blame-all . . . ," p. 31), May 1734 (ch. 7, "Where there's marriage
. . . ," p. 177), June 1734 (ch. 11, "Would you persuade . . . ," p. 247), April 1735
(ch. 11, "Necessity never . . . ," p. 242), July 1735 (ch. 4, "Three may keep . . . ,"
p. 106), September 1735 (ch. 13, "There is no . . . ," p. 280), June 1738 (ch. 7,
"Keep your eyes . . . ," p. 160), January 1746 ("When the well's . . . ," p. 11),
June 1746 (ch. 1, "Dost thou love . . . ," p. 43), April 1751 (ch. 1, "Most people
return . . . ," p. 55).

Don Fraser: Reader's Digest, *Quotable Quotes,* 1997 (ch. 7, 164).

Robert Frost:
interview in *Writers at Work,* 2nd series, 1963 (ch. 9, p. 194).
lecture at Milton Academy (Massachusetts), May 17, 1935 (ch. 11, p. 251).

James Anthony Froude: "Party Politics," *Short Stories on Great Subjects,* third series
(chs. 1, p. 53; 9, p. 204).

Margaret Fuller: "Diary," from Thomas Wentworth Higginson, *Life of Margaret Fuller
Ossoli,* 1884, ch. 18 (ch. 6, p. 152).

Thomas Fuller:
"Fame," *The Holy State and the Profane State,* 1642 (ch. 7, "Fame sometimes . . . ,"
p. 174).
The Holy State and the Profane State, 1642 (chs. 2, p. 73; 4, p. 113 and 11
["Learning hath . . . ," p. 239]).
Gnomologia: Adages and Proverbs, 1732 (chs. 1, p. 37; 9, p. 197 ["He that has
no . . . "], and 11 ["Take care . . . "], p. 264), no. 2662 (ch. 9, "If a man once
fall . . . ," p. 198), no. 3674 (ch. 5, "Nothing sharpens . . . ," p. 133), no. 404
(ch. 9, "The small demerit . . . ," p. 210).
Introductio ad Prudentiam, 1731 (chs. 7 ["If a friend . . . ," p. 179] and 11
["Constant popping . . . "], p. 243).

Gabirol (Solomon ben Yehuda ibn Gabirol): *The Choice of Pearls,* c. 1050 |
(chs. 1, p. 42; 3, p. 82; 6, pp. 145, 147 ["A man's mind . . ." and "A wise
man's . . ."]).

Galen: *On the Natural Faculties,* c. 170, book 1, sect. 2 (ch. 1, p. 18).

Paul Gauguin: Quoted in Huneker, *Pathos of Distance,* 1913, p. 128 (ch. 11,
p. 252).

John Gay: "The Elephant and the Book Seller," *Fables,* 1727–1738 (ch. 10, p. 222).

André Gide:
Journals, 1930 (ch. 1, "Fish die . . . ," p. 37).
Journals, 1939–1950 (ch. 13, p. 284).
The Counterfeiters, 1926 (chs. 1 ["The most decisive . . . ," p. 59] and 9, p. 205).

Johann Wolfgang von Goethe:
Autobiography, 1811 (ch. 8, p. 189).

"Conversation with Johann Peter Eckermann," October 20, 1828 (ch. 1, "One must *be* something . . . ," p. 42).

Elective Affinities, 1809, (ch. 1, "Men show their . . . ," p. 23 and "A man's manners . . . ," p. 44).

Faust, 1806 (ch. 2, p. 77); *Iphigenia in Taurus,* 1787, act 1, scene 3 (ch. 4, "One says a lot . . . ," p. 110).

Kunst and Alterthum, 1816–1832 (ch. 11, "He who does not know . . . ," p. 258).

Maxims and Reflections, early nineteenth century (chs. 4 ["Against criticism . . . ," p. 114], 6 ["Only when we know . . . ," p. 146 "All intelligent thoughts . . . ," p. 150 and "All professional men . . . ," p. 156], 11 ["Doubt grows . . .," p. 248 and "Some books seem . . . ," p. 254], and 12 ["The century . . . "], p. 268).

Proverbs in Prose, 1819 (chs. 3, p. 82 and 6 ["Nothing is more . . . ," p. 157], 5 ["Everything that . . . ," p. 118], and 11 ["Individuality of . . . ,"] p. 250).

Oliver Goldsmith:

She Stoops to Conquer, 1773, act 2 (ch. 1, p. 59).

The Bee, 1759 (ch. 11, "True genius . . . ," p. 257 and "The true use of . . . ," p. 259).

E. H. Gombrich: *Art and Illusion,* 1960 (ch. 1, p. 36).

Paul Goodman: *Growing Up Absurd: Problems of Youth in the Organized Society,* 1956, (ch. 11, p. 232).

Baltasar Gracián: *The Art of Worldly Wisdom,* 1647 (chs. 2, p. 72; 3, p. 85; 7, p. 175 ["A beautiful woman . . ." and "Never have a . . .], 10, p. 218; 11, p. 254 and 12, p. 270).

Graham Greene: *The Heart of the Matter,* 1948, pt. 1, ch. 2, sect. 4 (ch. 3, p. 90).

Georg Groddeck: *The Book of the It,* 1950, letter 14 (ch. 1, p. 13).

Philip Guedalla: Quoted in Hugh Leonard, "Can a Playwright Truly Depict Himself?" *New York Times,* November 23, 1980 (ch. 11, p. 256).

Arthur Guiterman: In Kleinberg, *Prophets in Their Own Country,* 1992 (ch. 11, p. 261).

Sacha Guitry: *Toutes réflexions faites,* 1947 (ch. 3, p. 86).

Hannibal: Attributed (ch. 1, p. 61).

Thomas Hardy: F. E. Hardy, *The Later Years of Thomas Hardy,* 1930 (ch. 6, p. 151).

Richard Harkness: *New York Herald Tribune,* June 15, 1960 (ch. 1, p. 32).

A. Eustace Haydon: *Quest of the Ages,* 1929, p. 202 (ch. 10, p. 220).

William Hazlitt:

Characteristics, 1823 (chs. 5 ["It is well that . . . ," p. 120] and 11 ["Men of genius . . . "], p. 241).

Life of Napoleon Bonaparte, 1828–1830, vol. 4, p. 267 (ch. 2, p. 69).

Note-Books, 1856, p. 236 (ch. 5, "We are not satisfied . . . ," p. 118).

"On Prejudice," *Sketches and Essays,* 1839 (chs. 6, p. 155 and 10 ["Prejudice is the . . . ," p. 122]).

"On Taste," *Sketches and Essays,* 1839 (ch. 11, "Rules and models . . . ," p. 249).
"On the Clerical Character," *Political Essays,* 1819 (ch. 1, "Those who make . . . ," p. 25).
On the Knowledge of Character, 1822 (ch. 1, "The greatest grossness . . . ," p. 35).
On the Love of Life, 1815 (chs. 1, p. 51 and 13 ["Our repugnance . . . ,"287]).
Sketches and Essays, 1839 (chs. 1, p. 29 and 10 ["Without the aid . . . ," p. 216]).
The Spirit of Controversy, January 31, 1830 (ch. 11, "When a thing ceases . . . ," p. 237).
Georg Wilhelm Hegel: "Introduction," *Philosophy of History,* 1832 (ch. 3, p. 89); ch. 2, sect. 3, pt. 3 (ch. 10, p. 220).
Heinrich Heine: attributed (ch. 11, p. 246).
Joseph Heller: "Of Colonel Cargill," *Catch–22,* 1961, ch. 3 (ch. 2, p. 69).
Sir Arthur Helps:
    Essays Written in Intervals of Business, 1841 (ch. 1, "Remember that . . . ," p. 4).
    Friends in Council, book 2, chapter 1 (ch. 11, p. 247).
    Thoughts in the Cloister and the Crowd, 1835 (chs. 1 ["Many know how . . . ," p. 7] and 6, p. 141).
Claude Adrien Helvétius: "Preface," *De l'esprit,* 1758 (ch. 3, p. 83); *Notes, maxims, et pensées,* 1909 (ch. 5, p. 124).
Ernest Hemingway:
    interview in *Paris Review,* Spring 1958 (ch. 11, p. 255).
    remark to Marlene Dietrich, quoted in A. E. Hotchner, *Papa Hemingway: A Personal Memoir,* 1967, (ch. 1, p. 39).
Heraclitus:
    Fragment 60, reprinted in H. Diels and W. Kranz, *Die Fragmente der Vorsokratiker,* 1954 (ch. 1, p. 39).
    Fragments, c. 500 B.C., 12 (ch. 10, p. 227).
    On the Universe, 1.21 (ch. 2, p. 73).
George Herbert:
    Jacula Prudentum, 1651, no. 49 (ch. 7, p. 177), no. 141 (ch. 1, "Love your neighbor . . . ," p. 59), no. 153 (ch. 1, "The mill cannot . . . ," p. 55), no. 390 (ch. 1, "The buyer needs . . . ," p. 62), no. 524 (ch. 1, "Living well . . . ," p. 35), no. 652 (ch. 3), no. 723 (ch. 13, p. 288).
    Jacula Prudentum, 1651 (ch. 1, "The offender . . . ," p. 9 also expressed by John Dryden in *The Conquest of Granada*).
    "The Church Porch," *The Temple,* 1633, stanza 5 (ch. 1, "Drink not . . . ," p. 53).
Robert Herrick: *The End,* 1648 (ch. 1, p. 27).
Abraham Joshua Heschel: *The Insecurity of Freedom: Essays on Human Existence,* 1967, (ch. 1, p. 17).

Hesiod: *Works and Days,* 698, line I (ch. 1, p. 63).
Herman Hesse:
  Demian: The Story of Emil Sinclair's Youth, 1919, (ch. 10, p. 223).
  Siddhartha, Govinda, 1922 (ch. 6, p. 137).
Cullen Hightower: Reader's Digest, *Quotable Quotes,* 1997 (ch. 4, p. 105).
Eric Hoffer:
  Passionate State of Mind, 1955, p. 21 (ch. 1, "When people are . . . , p. 28), p. 217
    (ch. 5, "Our greatest pretenses . . . ," p. 121), p. 222 (ch. 1, "You can discover . . . ,"
    p. 12), p. 241 (chs. 1, p. 4 and 5, "Rudeness is . . . ," p. 118).
  The Ordeal of Change, 1963 (chs. 6, p. 147; 9, p. 199).
Hugo von Hofmannsthal: *The Book of Friends,* 1922 (ch. 6, p. 158).
Andrew J. Holmes: *Wisdom in Small Doses,* (ch. 1, p. 8).
Oliver Wendell Holmes Jr.: "Ideals and Doubts," *Illinois Law Review,* May 1915 (ch. 6,
    "To have doubted . . . ," p. 148).
Oliver Wendell Holmes Sr.: *The Autocrat of the Breakfast-Table,* 1858, ch. 2 (ch. 6,
    p. 150), ch. 6 (ch. 11, p. 232).
Homer:
  The Iliad, c. 750 B.C.E., book 1, l. 218 (ch. 8, p. 186).
  The Odyssey, book 2, l. 276 (ch. 9, p. 200), book 8, l. 392 (ch. 1, p. 61).
Sir Anthony Hope: *The Prisoner of Zenda,* ch. 1 (ch. 1, p. 29).
Jane Ellice Hopkins: *Work Amongst Working Men,* 1870 (ch. 6, p. 160).
Horace:
  Epistles, 13 B.C., book I, epistle 2, l. 40 (ch. 6, p. 160).
  Odes, 23 B.C., book 1, ode 4, l. 13 (ch. 1, "Pale Death . . . ," p. 27), book 1, ode 9, l.
    13 (ch. 2, "Cease to ask . . . ," p. 75).
  Satires, 35 B.C., book 1, satire 1, l. 117 (ch. 9, p. 197), book 1, satire 19, l. 2 (ch. 11,
    "No poems can . . . ," p. 262), book 2, satire 8 (ch. 1, "A host is like . . . ," p. 48),
    book 2, satire 8, l. 73 (ch. 11, "Adversity has . . . ," p. 263).
Stanley Horowitz: Reader's Digest, *Quotable Quotes,* 1997 (ch. 13, p. 285).
Edgar Watson Howe: *Country Town Sayings: A Collection of Paragraphs from the* Atchison
    Globe, 1911 (ch. 10, p. 214), p. 256 (ch. 13, p. 279).
James Howell: *Proverbs,* 1659 (chs. 1, p. 27; 13, p. 280).
Elbert Hubbard:
  Restated by Victor Grayson [1881–1920]: "Never explain: Your friends don't need it
    and your enemies won't believe it"); *A Thousand and One Epigrams,* 1911, p. 145
    (ch. 13, "Never explain . . . ," p. 283), p. 68 (ch. 8, p. 183).
  Roycraft Dictionary and Book of Epigrams, 1914 (ch. 6, p. 158).
  The Note Book, 1927 (ch. 1, "The greatest mistake . . . ," p. 17).
  The Philistine, 1909, vol. 25, p. 62 (ch. 1, "Cultivate only . . . ," p. 27).

Frank McKinney "Kin" Hubbard:
    Abe Martin's Broadcast, 1930 (chs. 1, p. 3 and 3 ["Nobody forgets . . . ," p. 79]).
    Comments of Abe Martin and His Neighbors, 1923 (ch. 11, p. 261).
    Hoss Sense and Nonsense, 1926 (ch. 1, "When a fellow . . . ," p. 22).
Victor Hugo:
"Conclusion," *Histoire d'un crime,* 1977 (ch. 6, p. 153).
    Les Misérables, 1862 (ch. 9), "Cosette," (ch. 1, "Great blunders . . . ," p. 54).
    Tas de Pierres, midnineteenth century (ch. 1, "*Friend* is sometimes . . . ," p. 63).
    Ruy Blas, 1838, act 3, scene 5 (ch. 1, "Popularity? . . . ," p. 25), act 2, scene 5 (ch. 8, p. 183).
    The Toilers of the Sea, 1866, pt. 1, book 6, ch. 6 (ch. 3, p. 90).
Joseph Hunter: Reader's Digest, *Quotable Quotes,* 1997 (ch. 10, p. 210).
Aldous Leonard Huxley:
    Beliefs, Ends, and Means: An Inquiry into the Nature of Ideals and into the Methods Employed for Their Realization, 1937 (ch. 6, "Most ignorance . . . ," p. 147).
    "Mr. Topes," in *Green Tunnels, Mortal Coils,* 1922 (ch. 6, "Most of one's life . . . ," p. 135).
    Texts and Pretexts, 1932, p. 5 (ch. 1, "Experience is not . . . ," p. 12).
    The Idea of Equality, Proper Studies, 1927 (ch. 1, "That all men . . . ," p. 7).
Thomas Henry Huxley:
    "On Elementary Instruction in Physiology," 1877, in *Collected Essays,* vol. 3, 1895 (ch. 11, p. 247).
    "On the Advisableness of Improving Natural Knowledge," 1866, in *Lay Sermons, Addresses and Reviews,* 1870 (ch. 6, p. 146).
Henrik Ibsen: *An Enemy of the People,* 1882 (ch. 1, p. 53).
William Dean Inge: *Wit and Wisdom of Dean Inge,* 1927 (ch. 1, p. 33).
Robert Ingersoll: "The New Testament," *Some Reasons Why,* 1881, pt. 8 (ch. 8, p. 185).
Raymond Inmon: Reader's Digest, *Quotable Quotes,* 1997 (ch. 13, p. 289).
Iphicrates: Apothegms, from *Plutarch* (ch. 9, p. 204).
Andrew Jackson: attributed (ch. 10, p. 227).
William James:
    Letters, 1896 (ch. 1, "I now perceive . . . ," p. 56).
    The Principles of Psychology, 1890, ch. 19 (ch. 11, p. 238), ch. 22 (ch. 6, p. 147).
    Varieties of Religious Experience, 1902 (ch. 1, "Our civilization . . . ," p. 40).
Thomas Jefferson:
    Letter to Tench Coxe, May 21, 1799, in *Writings of Thomas Jefferson,* 1896, vol. 7, p. 381 (ch. 12, p. 273).
    Notes on the State of Virginia, 1781–1785, (ch. 8, p. 188).

Saint Jerome:
  letter 3 (ch. 1, "The friendship . . . ," p. 58).
  letter 52 (ch. 11, "Avoid, as you . . . ," p. 233).
  letter 53 (ch. 11, "It is worse still . . . ," p. 245).
Douglas William Jerrold: "Meeting Troubles Halfway," *Wit and Opinions of Douglas Jerrold,* 1859 (ch. 1, p. 57).
Sarah Orne Jewett: *The Country of the Pointed Firs,* 1896, ch. 10 (ch. 4, p. 108).
Dr. Samuel Johnson:
  Boswell, Life of Johnson, July 20, 1763 (ch. 2, "You never find . . . ," p. 76), 1776 (ch. 5, "To act from . . . ," p. 124), April 10, 1778 (ch. 9, "Every man thinks . . . ," p. 194), "Referring to the Giant's Causeway," October 12, 1779 (ch. 1, "Worth seeing? . . . ," p. 44), 1779 (ch. 1, "A man who . . . ," p. 16), 1780 (ch. 1, "The applause . . . ," p. 64), March 1781 (ch. 1, "There are people . . . ," p. 63), May 15, 1783 (ch. 6, "Clear your mind . . . ," p. 152), 1783 (ch. 1, "As I know more . . . ," p. 9 and "A man may be . . . ," p. 50), June 1784 (ch. 6, "I have found . . . ," p. 159), 1791 (chs. 9 ["While grief . . . ," p. 191] and 7 ["To marry . . . ," p. 167]), "Recalling the Advice of a College Tutor," 1791 (ch. 11, "Read over . . . ," p. 250).
  Letters to the Earl of Chesterfield, May 9, 1778 (ch. 6, "Were it not . . . ," p. 153).
  Plan of an English Dictionary, 1747 (ch. 2, "Those that have done . . . ," p. 77).
  Rasselas, 1759 (ch. 6, "Nothing will ever . . . ," p. 155).
  The Adventurer, no. 84 (ch. 4, "Silence propagates . . . ," p. 105).
  The Idler, 1758 (chs. 1, p. 2 and 3 ["We are inclined . . . ," p. 3] and 1 ["There is no kind . . . ," p. 60]
  The Rambler, 1750 (ch. 1, "The love of life . . . ," p. 45), 1751 (ch. 1, "Those who do not . . . ," p. 15), March 23, 1751 (ch. 11, "No place affords . . . ," p. 262), no. 135, 1751 (ch. 1, "Almost all absurdity . . . ," p. 10), no. 178 (ch. 1, "The future . . . ," p. 32), 1750–1752 (chs. 1 ["There is not . . . ," p. 22] and 5 ["Almost every man . . . ," p. 122]).
  Works, 1787, vol. 11, p. 216 (ch. 4, "He who praises . . . ," p. 116).
Erica Jong:
  How to Save Your Own Life, 1977 (chs. 11 ["And the trouble . . . ," p. 232] and 13, p. 279).
  The First Ms. *Reader,* 1973 (ch. 11, "Everyone has . . . ," p. 234).
Ben Jonson:
  An Epistle Answering to One That Asked to be Sealed to the Tribe of Ben, 1640 (ch. 4, "Those that merely . . . ," p. 103).
  Every Man Out of His Humor, 1599, act 1, scene 1 (ch. 11, "Art hath . . . ," p. 264).
  Timber; Or, Discoveries, 1640 (chs. 9 ["Greatness of name . . .] and 11 ["Language most . . . , p. 249]), "Explorata" (ch. 1, "He knows not . . . ," p. 43), "Of Learning

to Read Well, Speak Well, and Write Well" (ch. 11, "There be some men . . . ,"
     p. 240).
To the Immortal Memory . . . of . . . Sir Lucius Carey and Sir H. Morison, 1640 (ch. 1,
     "In small proportions . . . ," p. 41).
Joseph Joubert: *Pensées,* 1842 (chs. 3, p. 87; 4 ["Words, like . . . ," p.108 and "Before
     using . . . ," p. 110], and 6, p. 147).
Carl Gustav Jung:
     Book review, 1934 (ch. 6, "The stacking . . . ," p. 154).
     Paracelsus, 1934 (ch. 9, p. 193).
     Psychological Types, 1921 (ch. 11, p. 244).
     Psychology and Religion, 1940 (ch. 6, "The educated man . . . ," p. 152).
"The Letters of Junius": *Public Advertiser,* letter 35, December 19, 1769 (ch. 12, p. 272).
Juvenal: *Satires,* c. 18 B.C.E., no. 1 (ch. 5, p. 127).
Lajos Kassak: *Contemporary Artists,* 1977 (ch. 11, p. 248).
Helen Keller: Reader's Digest, *Quotable Quotes,* 1997 (ch. 9, p. 195).
Thomas à Kempis: *Imitation of Christ,* c. 1420, book 1, ch. 3 (ch. 1, p. 18).
Jean Kerr: Quoted in Gerald Nachman, *San Francisco Chronicle,* September 22, 1983
     (ch. 13, p. 281).
Søren Kierkegaard: *Either/Or,* 1843 (ch. 1, 19); *Journal,* 1850 (ch. 9, p. 201).
Martin Luther King Jr.:
     quoted in Garrow, *Bearing the Cross,* 1986, p. 80 (ch. 10, "The arm of . . . ,"
          p. 218).
     "Letter from Birmingham Jail," April 16, 1963 (ch. 10, "The time . . . ," p. 217).
Rudyard Kipling:
     We and They, 1926 (ch. 1, p. 12).
     "False Dawn," *Plain Tales from the Hills,* 1888 (ch. 4, p. 110).
     "Three and—an Extra," *Plain Tales from the Hills,* 1888 (ch. 13, p. 286).
John Knox: Inscription on Reformation Monument, Geneva, Switzerland (ch. 8, p. 188).
Karl Kraus:
     Aphorisms and More Aphorisms, 1909 (ch. 6, p. 156).
     "Hollow Heads," *Half-Truths and One-and-a-Half Truths,* 1976 (ch. 11, "Journalists
          write . . . ," p. 263).
     Thomas S. Szasz, *Karl Kraus and the Soul-Doctors: A Pioneer Critic and His Criticism of
          Psychiatry and Psychoanalysis,* 1976, (ch. 11, "A journalist is . . . ," p. 249).
     "Not for the Woman," *Half-Truths and One-and-a-Half Truths* (ch. 7, p. 170).
Louis Kronenberger: *Company Manners,* 1954, 2.1 (ch. 2, p. 72), 3.3 (ch. 1, p. 56).
Sir Roger L'Estrange: *Aesop's Fables,* 1692, (ch. 5, 130).
Jean de La Bruyère: *Characters,* 1688 (chs. 2 ["All men's . . . ," p. 74] and 7 ["It is
     because . . . ,"] p. 174), "Of Fashion" (ch. 5, p. 123), "Of Free-Thinkers" (ch. 8, p.

187), "Of Man" (ch. 9, "Most men make . . . ," p. 209), "Of Mankind" (chs. 1 ["We seek our . . . ," p. 14] and 11, p. 236), "Of Opinions" (ch. 4, p. 113), "Of the Affections" (ch. 6, p. 141), "Of the Court" (chs. 1 ["Life at court . . . ," p. 29], 2 ["The slave has . . . ," p. 71], and 3, p. 84), "Of the Gifts of Fortune" (ch. 2, "The shortest . . . ," p. 74), "Of Women" (chs. 7 ["A man keeps . . . ," p. 173] and 9 ["Women run . . . ,"] p. 205).

Jean de La Fontaine:
  Fables, 1668 (ch. 3, p. 81).
  "The Fox and the Crow," *Fables,* 1668 (ch. 4, p. 105).

Charles Varlet Marquis de La Grange: *Pensées,* 1872 (chs. 1, 4 ["We recognize . . ." and "When we ask . . . ,"] p. 2, p. 95, and 10, p. 227).

Jean-François de La Harpe: *Melanie,* 1770 (chs. 4, p. 107; 10, p. 214).

François, Duc de La Rochefoucauld:
  Maxims, 1665 (chs. 1 ["We often irritate . . . ," p. 42], 3 ["Our enemies' . . . ," p. 80 and "Almost all our . . . ," p. 85], 4 ["Sometimes we think . . . ," p. 111], 5 ["In the human heart . . . ," p. 121 "When the vices . . . ," p. 132 "We often pride . . . ," p. 126 and "In jealousy . . . ," p. 118], 7 ["The violence we do . . . ," p. 167], 9 ["Our enemies approach . . . ," p. 209]
  Maxims, 1678, no. 2 (ch. 1, "Self-love is . . . ," p. 18), no. 19 (ch. 2, "We all have . . . ," p. 75), no. 25 (ch. 2, "We need greater . . . ," p. 70), no. 31 (chs. 5 and 10, "If we had no faults . . . ," p. 121, 215), no. 32 (ch. 5, "Jealousy feeds . . . ", p. 131), no. 70 (ch. 7, "There is no disguise . . . ," p. 174), no. 71 (ch. 7, "There are very few . . . ," p. 171), no. 76 (ch. 7, "True love is . . . ," p. 165), no. 127 (ch. 3, "The true way . . . ," p. 90), no. 146 (ch. 4, "Usually we praise . . . ," p. 97), no. 149 (ch. 4, "To refuse praise . . . ," p. 100), no. 180 (ch. 1, "Our repentance . . . ," p. 20), no. 209 (ch. 6, "Who lives without . . . ," p. 154), no. 216 (ch. 5, "Perfect courage . . . ," p. 125), no. 226 (ch. 13, "Too great haste . . . ," p. 284), no. 245 (ch. 3, "The height of . . . ," p. 79 and "There is great . . . ," p. 92), no. 257 (ch. 5, "Solemnity is . . . ," p. 122), no. 276 (ch. 5, "Absence diminishes . . . ," p. 129), no. 294 (ch. 1, "We always like . . . ," p. 57), no. 298 (ch. 1, "The gratitude . . . ," p. 59), no. 304 (ch. 9, "We frequently . . . ," p. 197), no. 312 (ch. 4, "Lovers never get . . . ," p. 99), no. 327 (chs. 3 and 4, "We confess to . . . ," p. 81), no. 361 (chs. 5 and 7, "Jealousy is always . . . ," p. 132, 178), no. 375 (ch. 6, "Mediocre minds . . . ," p. 139), no. 377 (ch. 13, "The greatest fault . . . ," p. 288), no. 431 (ch. 1, "Nothing so much . . . ," p. 16), no. 471 (ch. 7, "In their first passion . . . ," p. 166), no. 487 (ch. 6, "Our minds are . . . ," p. 147), no. 496 (ch. 7, "Quarrels would not . . . ," p. 168), no. 583 (ch. 7, "In the misfortune . . . ," p. 166).

Marguerite de La Sablière: *Pensées,* c. late 17th century (ch. 5, p. 121).

Eugene Labiche: *Les vivacités du Capitaine Tic,* 1861 (ch. 3, p. 83).

Jean Baptiste Lamarck: *Philosophie zoologique,* 1809, pt. 2, ch. 7 (ch. 1, p. 28).

Charles Lamb: *Table Talk by the Late Elia,* in *The Athenaeum,* January 4, 1834
　　(ch. 1, p. 21).

Ann Landers: Attributed (ch. 11, p. 260).

Walter Savage Landor: "Martin and Jack," *Imaginary Conversations,* 1824–1829 (ch. 8,
　　p. 187).

Doug Larson: United Feature Syndicate (ch. 7, p. 167).

Johann Kasper Lavater: *Aphorisms on Man,* c. 1788, no. 157 (chs. 1, p. 18;
　　4, p. 96).

David Herbert Lawrence:
　　"All Knowing," *Pansies,* 1929 (ch. 6, "It's bad taste . . . ," p. 147), "Peace and War"
　　　　(ch. 6, "All that we know . . . ," p. 160).
　　John Galsworthy, 1927 (ch. 6, "The more scholastically . . . ," p. 153).
　　White Peacock, 1911, pt. 2, ch. 2 (ch. 1, "Be a good animal . . . ," p. 40).

Fran Lebowitz: "People," *Social Studies,* 1981 (chs. 1, p. 3; 4, p. 95).

Abbott Joseph Liebling: "Do You Belong in Journalism?" *New Yorker,* May 4, 1960
　　(ch. 12, p. 269).

Stanislaw Jerzy Lec: *Unkempt Thoughts,* 1962, (chs. 1, p. 24; 12, p. 273).

Rosamond Lehmann: *The Ballad and the Source,* 1945 (ch. 11, p. 264).

Count Giacomo Leopardi: *Pensieri,* 1834–1837 (ch. 3, p. 92).

Gotthold Ephraim Lessing: *Emilia Golotti,* 1772, (ch. 6, p. 158).

Ada Leverson:
　　Love's Shadow, 1908 (ch. 7, "As a rule . . . ," p. 164).
　　Tenterhooks, 1912, ch. 7 (ch. 7, "You don't know . . . ," p. 171).

Georg Christoph Lichtenberg:
　　Aphorisms, 1764–1799 (chs. 1 ["To do just . . . ," p. 27], 6 ["There are people . . . ,"
　　　　p. 142], and 11 ["A book is a . . . ," p. 259 and "Reading means . . . ," p. 236],
　　　　"Notebook J," c. 1791 (ch. 1, "It is a golden . . . ," p. 3), "Notebook L," c. 1791
　　　　(ch. 6, "With most men . . . ," p. 138).

Charles Joseph, Prince de Ligne: *Mes écarts,* 1796 (ch. 1, p. 19).

John Locke: *An Essay Concerning Human Understanding,* 1894, (ch. 3, p. 91).

David Lodge: *The British Museum Is Falling Down,* 1965, ch. 4 (ch. 11, p. 255).

Friedrich von Logau: "Retribution," *Poetic Aphorisms,* 1654 (ch. 8, p. 184).

Jack London: "Editor's Note" by Douglas Brinkley, in Hunter S. Thompson, *The Proud
　　Highway: Saga of a Desperate Southern Gentleman, 1955–1967,* 1997 (ch. 11,
　　p. 235).

Henry Wadsworth Longfellow: *Kavanagh,* 1849, book 1, ch. 1 (chs. 1, p. 58; 10, p. 212);
　　Morituri Salutamus, 1875, stanza 9 (ch. 12, p. 269).

James Russell Lowell:
  A Fable for Critics, 1848 (ch. 1, "In creating . . . ," p. 35).
  "Cambridge Thirty Years Ago," *Literary Essays,* 1864–1890, vol. 1 (ch. 10, p. 221).
  "Democracy Address," Birmingham, England, October 6, 1884 (ch. 1, "Whatever you may . . . ," p. 51).
  My Study Windows, 1871 (ch. 7, p.177).
Clare Booth Luce: *Wit and Wisdom of Famous American Women,* 1986 (ch. 11, p. 251).
Lucretius: *De Rerum Natura* (On the Nature of Things), first century B.C., book 5 (ch. 1, p. 24), book 3, l. 55 (ch. 9, p. 210).
Joseph Russell Lynes, Jr.: "To the American Association of Advertising Agencies," April 25, 1963 (ch. 6, p. 152).
Hugh MacDiarmid: "Sayings of the Week," *Observer,* March 29, 1953 (ch. 11, p. 251).
Niccolò Machiavelli: *The Prince,* 1517 (ch. 2, p. 75).
Sir Compton Mackenzie: *Literature in My Time,* 1933, ch. 22 (ch. 1, p. 10).
Norman Mailer: *Writers at Work,* 3rd series (ch. 11, p. 234).
Robert Mallett: *Apostilles,* 1972 (chs. 1 ["How many pessimists . . . ," p. 6], 2, p. 70 and 6, p. 161).
Ruby Manikan: "Sayings of the Week," *Observer,* March 30, 1947 (ch. 11, p. 253 echoing Bishop Fenelon's treatise on the education of girls).
Thomas Mann: "Tonio Kroger," *Death in Venice,* 1903 (ch. 7, p. 165).
Lord William Murray Mansfield: John Lord Campbell, *The Lives of the Chief Justices of England,* 1849, vol. 2, ch. 40 (ch. 10, p. 213).
Donald Robert Perry Marquis: "A Farewell," *Archy Does His Part,* 1935 (ch. 7, p. 172).
Philip Massinger: *The Bondman,* 1623, act 1, scene 3 (ch. 12, p. 273).
Henri Matisse: *New York Times,* 1948 (ch. 11, p. 243).
William Somerset Maugham:
  Of Human Bondage, 1915, ch. 15 (ch. 1, p. 4).
  The Summing Up, 1938, ch. 15 (chs. 5, p. 127; 9, p. 194).
Charles Maurice, Prince de Talleyrand-Périgord: Reader's Digest, *Quotable Quotes,* 1997 (chs. 1, p. 34; 13, p. 282).
André Maurois:
  Ariel, 1924, ch. 12 (ch. 5, p. 124).
  De la conversation, 1921 (ch. 6, p. 151).
Mary Therese McCarthy: "The American Realist Playwrights," *On the Contrary,* 1961 (ch. 6, p. 140).
William McFee: *Casuals of the Sea,* 1916, act 2, scene 1, l. 6 (ch. 2, p. 70).
Margaret Mead: Speech to the National Council of Women, New York City, April 16, 1975 (ch. 13, p. 279).
Herman Melville: *Pierre,* 1952 (ch. 3, p. 90).

Menander of Athens: *The Girl Who Gets Flogged,* fragment 422 (ch. 11, p. 236).
Henry Louis Mencken:
  A Little Book in C Major, 1916, (chs. 1, p. 4 and 3 ["It is hard to . . . ," p. 79]), p. 59
    (ch. 7, "On one issue . . . ," p. 167).
  "Footnote on Criticism," *Prejudices,* 3rd series, 1922 (ch. 1, "Injustice is . . . ," p. 31).
  Minority Report: Notebooks, 1956 (ch. 3, "No man of honor . . . ," p. 80).
  "Sententiae," *A Book of Burlesques,* 1920 (ch. 7, "Adultery is . . . ," p. 179).
  "Sententiae," *This and That: A Mencken Chrestomathy,* 1949 (chs. 1 ["Conscience
    is . . . ," p. 4] and 6, p. 135).
  "The Blushful Mystery: Art and Sex," *Prejudices,* 1st series, 1919 (ch. 11, p. 265).
George Meredith:
  Diana of the Crossways, 1885, ch. 1 (ch. 13, p. 286).
  The Ordeal of Richard Feverel, 1859, ch. 34 (chs. 4, p. 104; 11, p. 244).
Gabriel Meurier: *Trésor des sentences,* (ch. 4, p. 116).
John Stuart Mill: *Bentham,* 1838 (ch. 6, p. 142).
Olin Miller: *Reader's Digest,* June 1939 (ch. 13, p. 279).
John Milton:
  Paradise Lost, 1667 (ch. 5, p. 127), book 1, l. 648 (ch. 10, p. 229).
  Paradise Regained, 1671, book 4, l. 327 (ch. 11, p. 236).
  Tenure of Kings and Magistrates, 1649 (ch. 12, p. 276).
Mistinguett: *Theatre Arts,* December 1955 (ch. 7, p. 165).
Joni Mitchell: Interview on BBC Television, 1985 (ch. 11, p. 258).
Wilson Mizner: Quoted in Alva Johnston, *The Legendary Mizners,* 1953, ch. 4 (ch. 11,
    p. 248).
Jean Baptiste Poqurlin Molière: *Amphitryon,* 1666, act 1, scene 4 (ch. 5); *Tartuffe,* 1664,
    act 1, scene 1 (ch. 4, p. 112).
Charles Edward Montague: *Disenchantment,* 1922, ch. 16 (ch. 12, p. 270).
Michel Eyquem de Montaigne:
  "Of Prayers," *Essays,* 1580–1588, "A Custom of the Isle of Cea" (ch. 6, "A wise
    man . . . ," p. 140), "Of Pedantry" (ch. 6, "We should rather . . . ," p. 156).
  Essays, 1595, book 3, ch. 1 (chs. 1 ["Few men have . . . "], 4, p. 103 and 5, p. 127).
Charles Louis de Secondat, Baron de Montesquieu:
  Pensées et Jugements, 1899 (ch. 13, p. 285).
  Mes pensées, c. 1722–1755 (ch. 1, "Mediocrity is . . . ," p. 14).
George Moore: "Mummer-worship," *Impressions and Opinions,* 1891 (ch. 11, p. 238).
Christopher Morley: *Where the Blue Begins,* 1922, p. 85 (ch. 9, p. 205).
Robert Morley: "Sayings of the Week," *Observer,* December 6, 1964 (ch. 4, p. 102).
Raymond Mortimer: Reader's Digest, *Quotable Quotes,* 1977 (ch. 13, p. 281).
Mr. Tut-Tut: *Chinese, A Night's Tale,* seventeenth century (ch. 6, p. 146).

Edward R. Murrow: December 31, 1955 (ch. 10, p. 228).

Robert von Musil: *Kleine Prosa,* c. 1930 (ch. 1, p. 46).

Napoleon I: *Maxims,* early nineteenth century (ch. 4, "The best way . . . ," p. 101 and "He who knows . . . ," p. 114).

José Narosky: Reader's Digest, *Quotable Quotes,* 1997 (ch. 12, p. 269).

John Neal: Reader's Digest, *Quotable Quotes,* 1997 (ch. 10, p. 226).

Sir Isaac Newton: *Reader's Digest,* October 1946 (ch. 13, p. 281).

Friedrich Wilhelm Nietzsche:

   Assorted Opinions and Maxims, 1879, aphorism 335 (ch. 1, "On the heights . . . ," p. 23), aphorism 340 (ch. 4, "So long as men . . . ," p. 95), aphorism 6 (ch. 3, "The visionary . . . ," p. 88).

   Beyond Good and Evil, 1886 (chs. 3 ["Success has . . . ," p. 79]).

   Human, All Too Human, 1878–1886 (ch. 3, "Convictions are . . . ," p. 86).

   "On the Pitying," *Thus Spake Zarathustra,* 1883–1885, (ch. 1, "Beggars should . . . ," p. 15).

   The Gay Science, 1882–1887 (chs. 1 ["Possessions are . . . ," p. 54 and "It is easier . . . ," p. 55] and 5 ["At times . . . ," p. 130]).

   The Twilight of the Idols, 1888, (ch. 11, "What does . . . ," p. 237 and "For art to exist . . . ," p. 248).

   Thus Spake Zarathustra, 1883–1885 (ch. 9, p. 195).

Anaïs Nin: *The Diary of Anaïs Nin,* 1966–1971 (ch. 10, p. 225).

Red O'Donnell: Reader's Digest, *Quotable Quotes,* 1997 (ch. 9, p. 208).

Aristotle Onassis: *The Economist,* November 1991 (ch. 11, p. 242).

George Orwell: *Animal Farm,* 1945, ch. 10 (chs. 1, p. 33; 12, p. 277).

Sir William Osler: *Montreal Medical Journal,* September 1902 (ch. 6, "The greater . . . ," p. 160).

Peter Ouspensky: *The Psychology of Man's Possible Evolution,* 1954, ch. 2 (ch. 3, p. 90).

Ovid: *Ars Amatoria,* book 3, 1. 425 (chs. 10, p. 233; 13, p. 281).

Vilfredo Pareto: Comment on Kepler (ch. 3, p. 88).

Dorothy Parker:

   "Ballade of a Great Weariness," *Enough Rope,* 1927, stanza 1 (ch. 7, p. 169).

   interview by Marion Capron, 1956, in *Writers at Work,* 1st series, 1958 (ch. 13, p. 288).

Cyril Northcote Parkinson: *Inlaws and Outlaws,* 1962 (ch. 11, p. 265).

Blaise Pascal:

   Letters provinciales, 1656–1657, no. 16 (ch. 11, "I have made . . . ," p. 262), no. 4 (ch. 1, "Things are always . . . ," p. 59).

   Pensées, 1654–1662 no. 384 (ch. 3, p. 87).

   Pensées, 1654–1662, pt. 1, no. 7 (ch. 6, "The more intelligent . . . ," p. 141).

Pensées, 1670 (chs. 4 ["We are generally . . . ," p. 97], 6 ["Man is equally . . . ," p. 153], and 11 ["When some passion . . . ," p. 245]), no. 29 (ch. 11, "When we see . . . ," p. 253), no. 101 (ch. 7, "If all persons . . . ," p. 176), no. 139 (ch. 1, "All the trouble . . . ," p. 59), no. 352 (ch. 5, "The strength of . . . ," p. 133), no. 430 (ch. 1, "To ridicule . . . ," p. 34), no. 513 (ch. 12, "The world is ruled . . . ," p. 270).
Louis Pasteur: Inaugural lecture, University of Lille, December 7, 1854 (ch. 2, p. 74).
George Smith Patton:
  Reader's Digest, *Quotable Quotes,* 1997 (ch. 9, "Success is how . . . ," p. 193).
  Bottom Line Personal, November 1996 (ch. 10, p. 226).
  War as I Knew It, 1947 (ch. 9, "Never tell people . . . ," p. 209).
Luciano Pavarotti: Reader's Digest, *Quotable Quotes,* 1997 (ch. 9, p. 199).
Cesare Pavese: *This Business of Living: Diaries, 1935–1950,* (chs. 1, p. 41; 11, p. 240).
William Penn: *Some Fruits of Solitude,* 1693 (chs. 1, p. 3; 12, p. 277).
Pericles: Plutarch, "Pericles," *Lives of the Philosophers,* sect. 18 (ch. 1, p. 41).
Maxwell Perkins: Said to Marsha Davenport, (ch. 11, p. 247).
Petrarch:
  Des remedies, 1366, book 2 (ch. 5, p. 129).
  To Laura in Death, canzone 137 (ch. 7, p. 176).
Plato:
  Laws, book 7, 816–B (ch. 6, p. 144).
  The Republic, book 1, 343–D (ch. 12, "When there is . . . ," p. 274), 377–B (ch. 1, "The beginning is . . . ," p. 51), book 3, 413–C (ch. 3, p. 89), book 7, 537 (ch. 11, p. 233), book 8, 562–A (ch. 12, "Democracy passes . . . ," p. 272), book 10, 601–D (ch. 1, "No human thing . . . ," p. 10).
Titus Maccius Plautus:
  Miles Gloriosus, act 3, scene 1 (ch. 1, p. 62).
  Trinummus, act 2, scene 2, l. 48 (ch. 9, p. 207).
Pliny the Younger: *Letters,* book 2, letter 15 (ch. 1, p. 64).
Alexander Pope:
  Eloisa to Abelard, 1717, l. 215 (ch. 7, p. 163).
  The Temple of Fame, 1711 (ch. 4, "And all who told . . . ," p. 113).
  "Thoughts on Various Subjects," in Swift, *Miscellanies,* 1727 (chs. 4 ["Who are next . . . ," p. 100], 5, p. 120; 6, p. 151 and 8, p. 185).
Neil Postman: "Introduction," *The Disappearance of Childhood,* 1982 (ch. 9, p. 193).
Ezra Pound: "Warning," *ABC of Reading,* 1934 (ch. 11, p. 260).
Matthew Prior: *Upon This Passage in Scaligerana,* 1697 (ch. 4, p. 100).
Marcel Proust:
  The Fugitive, Remembrance of Things Past, 1925 (ch. 7, "It is seldom . . . ," p. 170).
  The Past Recaptured, Remembrance of Things Past, 1913–1927 (ch. 9, p. 204).

Time Regained, Remembrance of Things Past, 1927 (ch. 7, "A woman we . . . ," p. 178).
Within a Budding Grove, Remembrance of Things Past, 1919 (chs. 4 ["A powerful
    idea . . . ," p. 104], 6 ["All our final . . . ," p. 140], and 7 ["There can be . . . ," p. 170
    and "It is a mistake . . . ," p. 179]).
Arthur Radford: "Admiral," in "Man Behind the Power," *Time,* February 25, 1957 (ch. 11,
    p. 241).
Ayn Rand: *The Ayn Rand Letter,* 1971 (ch. 1, p. 30).
Arthur Ransome: *We Didn't Mean to Go to Sea,* 1937 (ch. 11, p. 266).
John Ray: *English Proverbs,* 1670 (ch. 1, p. 58).
Jules Renard: *Journal,* 1890 (ch. 1, p. 46), 1898 (ch. 2, p. 75).
Jean François-Paul de Gandi, Cardinal de Retz: *Memoirs,* 1673–1676 (ch. 5, p. 119).
Robert Rice: *The Business of Crime,* 1956 (ch. 11, p. 239).
Johann Paul Friedrich Richter: *Flower, Fruit, and Thorn,* 1796–1797, (ch. 2, p. 68).
Nelson Rockefeller: Reader's Digest, Quotable Quotes, 1997 (ch. 10, p. 225).
Rutherford D. Rogers: *New York Times,* February 25, 1985 (ch. 6, p. 155).
Anna Eleanor Roosevelt: *The Wit and Wisdom of Eleanor Roosevelt,* 1996, p. 92 (ch. 1,
    p. 63).
Jean Rostand:
    Carnet d'un biologiste, 1962 (ch. 12, p. 268).
    De la vanité, 1925 (chs. 3, p. 83; 4, p. 96).
    Julien ou une conscience, 1928 (ch. 5, p. 129).
    Pensées d'un biologiste, 1939, p. 116 (ch. 10, p. 230).
Eddie Rickenbacker: *New York Times,* 1963 (ch. 10, p. 226).
Jean Jacques Rousseau:
    Discourse upon the Origin and Foundation of the Inequality Among Mankind, 1754 (ch.
    12, p. 276).
    Reader's Digest, *Quotable Quotes,* 1997 (ch. 4, p. 102).
Helen Rowland: *Reflections of a Bachelor Girl,* 1909 (chs. 5, p. 124; 7, p. 171).
Howard Ruff: *How to Prosper in the Coming Bad Years,* 1979 (ch. 1, p. 21).
John Ruskin: "Preface," *Sesame and Lilies,* 1865 (ch. 11, p. 235).
Bertrand Arthur William Russell:
    In MacIntosh, *Memoirs,* 1835, vol. 2, p. 473 (ch. 6, p. 160).
    Mysticism and Logic, 1918, ch. 4 (ch. 8, p. 189).
    On Education, 1926 (ch. 4, p. 96).
    Skeptical Essays, 1928, p. 109 (ch. 1, "The people who . . . ," p. 47).
    Unpopular Essays, 1950 (ch. 1, "The most savage . . . ," p. 33).
Mark Rutherford: *More Pages from a Journal,* 1910 (ch. 1, p. 55).
Joe Ryan: *Reader's Digest,* October 1961 (ch. 1, p. 30).
Sa'di (Musharrif-uddin): *Gulistan,* 1258, (ch. 1, p. 61).

Antoine de Saint-Exupéry: "Wind, Sand, and Stars," in *Terre des Hommes,* 1939,
    ch. 2, sect. 2 (ch. 1, p. 50).
Saki (Hector Hugh Monro):
    "Clovis on the Alleged Romance of Business," *The Square Egg,* 1924 (ch. 4, p. 104).
    "Reginald at the Carlton," *Reginald,* 1904 (ch. 9, p. 203).
    The Infernal Parliament, 1924 (ch. 1, p. 23).
Sallust: *The War with Catiline,* c. 40 B.C., ch. 10 (ch. 11, p. 242).
Lord Herbert Louis Samuel: *Reader's Digest,* September 1960 (ch. 12, p. 274).
Carl Sandburg: "Prairie", *Complete Poems,* 1950 (chs. 1, p. 34; 13, p. 288).
George Santayana: "War Shrines," *Soliloquies in England and Later Soliloquies,* 1922
    (chs. 1, p. 50; 9, p. 196); "Aversion from Platonism," *Soliloquies in England,* 1922
    (ch. 8, p. 186); "Reason in Common Sense," *The Life of Reason,* 1905–1906, vol. 1
    (chs. 5, p. 122; 7, p. 174 and 12, p. 269); *Skepticism and Animal Faith,* 1923, ch. 3
    (ch. 13, p. 282).
Jean Paul Sartre:
    Nausea, Monday, 1938 (ch. 3, p. 85).
    Situations, 1939, (ch. 1, p. 52).
George Savile, Marquess de Halifax:
    Complete Works, 1912, p. 12 (ch. 7, "A wife is to thank . . . ," p. 178), p. 252 (chs. 1
    and 6 ["Could we know . . . ," p. 20, p. 137]).
    Miscellaneous Thoughts and Reflections, late seventeenth century (chs. 4 ["Explaining
    is . . . ," p. 98 and "A fool hath . . . ," p. 106], 5 ["Our virtues and . . . ," p. 126],
    6 ["Nothing has an . . . ," p. 138 "A wise man . . . ," p. 139 and "Men who
    borrow . . . ," p. 144], and 11 ["Weak men are . . . ," p. 258]), "Of Company,"
    (ch. 1, "Men that cannot . . . ," p. 30).
    Political Thoughts and Reflections, 1687, "Of Punishment" (ch. 1, "Men are not
    hanged . . . ," p. 4), (ch. 11, "Men in business . . . ," p. 237).
    Political, Moral, and Miscellaneous Thoughts and Reflections, 1750 (chs. 4 ["Most men
    make . . . ," p. 108]
Johann Christoph Friedrich von Schiller:
    The Conspiracy of Fiesco, 1783, act 1, scene 7 (ch. 13, p. 284), act 1, scene 1 (ch. 7,
    p. 176).
    The Death of Wallenstein, 1798, act 1, scene 4 (ch. 1, "Many a crown . . . ," p. 58).
    The Piccolomini, 1799, act 2, scene 12 (ch. 1, "When the wine . . . ," p. 33).
    Wilhelm Tell, 1804, act 3, scene 1 (chs. 1 ["You saw his weakness . . . ," p. 64] and 6, p.
    136).
Arthur Schopenhauer:
    "Aphorisms on the Wisdom of Life," *Parerga and Paralipomena,* 1851 (ch. 1,
    "Scoundrels are . . . ," p. 16).

"Counsels and Maxims," *Parerga and Paralipomena,* 1851 (ch. 3, "If we suspect . . . ," p. 80).

"On the Doctrine of the Indestructibility of Our True Nature," *Parerga and Paralipomena,* 1851 (ch. 8, p. 184).

"What A Man Represents," *Parerga and Paralipomena,* 1851 (ch. 5, p. 124).

"Our Relations to Others," *Essays,* (ch. 6, "Intellect is . . . ," p. 154).

"Studies in Pessimism," *Psychological Observations,* 1851 (ch. 6, "Every man takes . . . ," p. 136).

Supplements to The World as Will and Idea (ch. 1, "Man is the only . . . ," p. 55).

Sir Walter Scott:

Marmion, 1808, (ch. 3, p. 91).

Quentia Durward, 1823 (chs. 4, p. 114; 13, p. 280).

Frank Scully: Reader's Digest, *Quotable Quotes,* 1997 (ch. 11, p. 249).

John Selden: "Bible, Humility," *Table Talk,* 1689 (ch. 5, "'Tis not the drinking . . . ," p. 122 and "Humility is . . . ," p. 123), "Bible, Learning" (chs. 1, p. 64; 6, p. 154; 11, p. 263 and 13, p. 287); *Table Talk,* 1689 (ch. 4, p. 100).

Lucius Annaeus Seneca:

Epistula ad Lucilium, epistle 29, (ch. 6, "What others think . . . ," p. 137).

Epistles, first century A.D. (ch. 4, "Nobody will keep . . . ," p. 98 and "You can tell . . . ," p. 113).

"On Tranquillity of the Mind," *Moral Essays,* (ch. 6, "There is no great . . . ," p. 159).

William Shakespeare:

Antony and Cleopatra, 1606–1607, act 1, scene 5, l. 73 (ch. 6, "My salad days . . . ," p. 156), act 22, scene 5, l. 85 (ch. 3, "Though it be . . . ," p. 92), act 3, scene 11, l. 94 (ch. 10, "Now he'll out stare . . . ," p. 225).

As You Like It, 1599–1600, act 1, scene 3, l. 123 (ch. 10, "We'll have a . . . ," p. 228), act 5, scene 1, l. 35 (ch. 6, "The fool doth . . . ," p. 156), act 5, scene 2, l. 48 (ch. 9, "Oh, what a bitter . . . ," p. 192).

Cymbeline, 1609–1610, act 3, scene 4 (ch. 7, "Men's vows are . . . ," p. 172), act 4, scene 3, l. 46 (ch. 2, "Fortune brings . . . ," p. 77).

Hamlet, 1600–1601, act 1, scene 3, l. 65 (ch. 1, "Beware of entrance . . . ," p. 63), act 2, scene 2, ll. 180–181 (ch. 5, "To be honest . . . ," p. 131), act 4, scene 5, l. 78 (ch. 9, "When sorrows come . . . ," p. 208).

King Henry the Eighth, 1613, act 4, scene 2, l. 45 (ch. 5, "Men's evil manners . . . ," p. 122).

King Henry the Fifth, 1598–1599, act 2, scene 4, l. 73–74 (ch. 9, "Self-love . . . ," p. 207).

King Henry the Sixth, 1590–1591, pt. 3, act 4, scene 7, l. 11 (ch. 1, "For many men . . . ," p. 7), act 2, scene 1, l. 85 (ch. 9, "To weep is to . . . ," p. 201).

King Lear, 1605, act 1, scene 4, l. 312 (ch. 9, "How sharper . . . ," p. 195), act 1, scene 4, l. 371 (ch. 2, "Striving to better . . . ," p. 77), act 4, scene 6, l. 187 (ch. 9, "When we are born . . . ," p. 205), act 5, scene 3 (ch. 1, "Jesters do oft . . . ," p. 58).

King Richard the Second, 1595, act 1, scene 3, l. 236 (ch. 1, "Things sweet . . . ," p. 26).

King Richard the Third, 1592–1593, act 1, scene 3, l. 351 (ch. 4, "Talkers are no . . . ," p. 103).

Measure for Measure, 1604, act 1, scene 4, l. 78 (ch. 10, "Our doubts are . . . ," p. 224), act 2, scene 1, l. 38 (ch. 2, "Some rise by sin . . . ," p. 70), act 5, scene 1, l. 440 (ch. 13, "They say best . . . ," p. 284).

Pericles (ch. 5, "Few love to . . . ," p. 124).

Romeo and Juliet, 1595–1596, act 3, scene 1 (ch. 8, "Mercy but murders . . . ," p. 182).

The Taming of the Shrew, 1593–1594, act 1, scene 1, l. 39 (ch. 10, "No profit grows . . . ," p. 219).

The Tempest, 1611–1612, act 2, scene 1, l. 261 (ch. 11, "What's past is . . . ," p. 259), act 2, scene 2, l. 42 (ch. 9, "Misery acquaints . . . ," p. 209).

Timon of Athens, 1605–1608, act 3, scene 5, l. 3 (ch. 8, "Nothing emboldens . . . ," p. 183).

George Bernard Shaw:
Back to Methuselah, 1921 (ch. 4, "Silence is . . . ," p. 106).

Caesar and Cleopatra, 1901, act 3 (ch. 13, "When a stupid . . . ," p. 281).

Candida, 1898, act 1 (chs. 1 ["We have no . . . ," p. 11] and 13 ["It is easy . . . ," p. 280]).

"Hearth and Home," *Getting Married,* 1911 (ch. 7, "Home life as . . . ," p. 173).

Days with Bernard Shaw, 1949 (ch. 12, "Power does not . . . ," p. 271).

Major Barbara, 1905, 3 (ch. 1, "You cannot have . . . ," p. 17).

Man and Superman, 1905, act 3 (ch. 11, "Hell is full . . .," p. 249 and "Music is . . . ," p. 262), act 4 (ch. 9, "Life contains . . . ," p. 192), "Maxims for Revolutionists: Reason" (ch. 6, "The man who . . . ," p. 149), "Maxims: Education" (ch. 12, "Democracy substitutes . . . ," p. 276), "Maxims: Liberty and Equality" (ch. 10, "Liberty means . . . ," p. 221), "The Revolutionist's Handbook" (ch. 1, "Gambling promises . . . ," p. 248).

"Preface on Doctors: Fashions and Epidemics," *The Doctor's Dilemma,* 1906 (ch. 1, "A fashion is . . . ," p. 28).

The Philanderer, 1893, act 4 (ch. 9, "The test of a . . . ," p. 206).

The Rejected Statement, pt. 1 (chs. 1, p. 30 and 12 ["Assassination is . . . ," p. 274]).

John A. Shedd: *Salt from My Attic,* (ch. 9, p. 191).

Gail Sheehy: *Passages,* 1976 (ch. 10, p. 225).

William Shenstone: *Essays on Men and Manners,* 1764 (chs. 5 ["A man has . . . ," p. 119 and "Jealousy is . . . ," p. 131] and 11).

Richard Brinsley Sheridan: Attributed—to a young lady (ch. 1, p. 32); *The Critic,* 1779, (ch. 5, p. 120).

Walter Richard Sickert: "The Language of Art," *New Age,* July 28, 1910 (ch. 1, "Nothing knits man . . . ," p. 7).

Beverly Sills: Reader's Digest, *Quotable Quotes,* 1979 (ch. 1, p. 60).

Cornelia Otis Skinner: Attributed (ch. 5, "Women's virtue . . . ," p. 131).

Logan Pearsall Smith:
 "All Trivia," *Afterthoughts,* 1931 (chs. 7, p. 176; 11, p. 235).
 "Life and Human Nature," *Afterthoughts,* 1931 (ch. 1, "There are few . . . ," p. 46).

Sydney Smith: letter to Bishop Blomfield, (ch. 5, p. 130).
 Reader's Digest, April 1952 (ch. 11, p. 257).
 "Recipe for Salad," *Lady Holland's Memoir,* 1855 (ch 9, "That sign of . . . ," p. 203).

Socrates: Quoted in Plato, *Apology,* 38a (ch. 1, p. 38).

Alexander Isayevich Solzhenitsyn: *The First Circle,* 1968 (ch. 12, p. 275).

William Somerville: *Ready Money,* 1727 (ch. 10, p. 223).

Susan Sontag: *Esquire,* 1968 (ch. 10, p. 229).

Sophocles:
 Acrisius, fragment 58 (ch. 1, "To the man . . . ," p. 6).
 Ajax, 440 B.C.E., l. 964 (ch. 1, "Men of ill . . . ," p. 38).
 Aletes, fifth century B.C., l. 99 (ch. 9, p. 203).
 Oedipus Rex, l. 1231 (ch. 1, "The keenest sorrow . . . ," p. 9).

Julia Sorel: *See How She Runs,* 1978 (ch. 11, p. 252).

Robert Southey: Reader's Digest, *Quotable Quotes,* 1997 (ch. 11, p. 261).

Herbert Spencer:
 "Prison Ethics," *Essays,* 1892, vol. 3 (ch. 13, p. 289).
 Social Statics, 1850, pt. 4, ch. 30, sect. 8 (ch. 1, p. 32).

Edmund Spenser: *The Faerie Queen,* 1596, book 6, canto 3, stanza 1 (ch. 1, p. 21).

Benedict Spinoza: *Ethics,* 1883, vol. 3, proposition 29 (ch. 5, "Those who are . . . ," p. 118), 4 appendix 21 (ch. 4, p. 98), 4 proposition 18 (ch. 5, "An emotion ceases . . . ," p. 123).

Charles Haddon Spurgeon: Reader's Digest, *Quotable Quotes,* 1997 (ch. 9, p. 210).

Anne Louise Germaine de Staël: *De l'influence des passions,* 1796 (ch. 7, p. 173).

Edwin McMasters Stanton: Attributed (ch. 1, p. 49; some credit this quote to Abraham Lincoln, who told an inquisitive cabinet member, "Every man over forty is responsible for his face," after turning down an older job applicant whose facial appearance he didn't like).

Sir Richard Steele: *The Spectator,* no. 497, September 30, 1712 (ch. 1, p. 19).

James Fitzjames Stephen: Attributed (ch. 11, p. 244).

Laurence Sterne: *Sermons,* 1760, vol. 1, no. 12 (ch. 10, p. 227); *Tristram Shandy,* 1760, book 2, ch. 3 (ch. 11, p. 237).

Adlai Stevenson: Speech, Springfield, Illinois, January 1951 (ch. 3, p. 83, p. 84).

Robert Louis Stevenson: "An Apology for Idlers," *Virginibus Puerisque,* 1881 (ch. 11, "Books are good . . . ," p. 250 and "Perpetual devotion . . . ," p. 242), "Crabbed Age and Youth" (ch. 9, p. 208).

Sir John Suckling: *Sonnet,* c. 1638, no. 2 (ch. 1, p. 50).

Sun-tzu: "Emptiness and Fullness," *The Art of War,* c. 375 B.C.E. (ch. 12, "Be extremely subtle . . . ," p. 277), "Strategic Assessments" (ch. 12, "A military operation . . . ," p. 271 and "Victorious warriors . . . ," p. 274).

Jonathan Swift:
A Critical Essay upon the Faculties of the Mind, 1707 (ch. 12, p. 273).
"Thoughts on Various Subjects," *Miscellanies,* 1711 (chs. 6, p. 135; 8, p. 184).

Herbert Bayard Swope: Speech, St. Louis, December 20, 1950 (ch. 2, p. 71).

Publilius Syrus:
Maxim 185, first century B.C. (ch. 11, p. 265), maxim 358 (ch. 1, "Anyone can hold . . . ," p. 65), maxim 402 (ch. 1, "Treat your friend . . . ," p. 61), maxim 511 (ch. 9, p. 195), maxim 6 (ch. 1, "He gives twice . . . ," p. 23).
Sententiae, c. 50 B.C. (ch. 3, p. 85).

Thomas Szasz: "Personal Conduct," *The Second Sin,* 1973 (chs. 1, p. 45; 6, p. 157).

Albert von Szent-Gyorgyi: In Foster, *Innovation,* 1980, p. 82 (ch. 6, p. 135).

Cornelius Tacitus:
Annals, early second century (ch. 1, "To show resentment . . . ," p. 60).
Histories, 115–116, book 3, ch. 86 (ch. 2, p. 74), book 4, ch. 6 (ch. 1, "Love of fame . . . ," p. 25).

Sir Rabindranath Tagore: *Stray Birds,* 1916 (ch. 3, p. 87); "The Judge," *The Crescent Moon,* 1913 (ch. 4, p. 115).

Booth Tarkington: *Penrod,* 1914, ch. 10 (ch. 1, p. 49).

Sir Henry Taylor: *The Statesman,* 1836 (chs. 4, p. 98; 6, p. 139).

Alfred Lord Tennyson: "Lancelot and Elaine," *Idylls of the King,* 1859–1885, l. 1082 (ch. 1, p. 62), "The Last Tournament," l. 652 (ch. 4, p. 96).

Quintus Septimus Tertullian:
Adversus Valentinianos, (ch. 3, "Truth does not . . . ," p. 89).
De Carne Christi, (ch. 3, "It is to be believed . . . ," p. 88).

Henry David Thoreau:
A Life Without Principle, 1863 (ch. 9, "There is no more . . . ," p. 210).
A Week on the Concord and Merrimack Rivers, 1849, Wednesday (ch. 9, "We are always . . . ," p. 210).

"Economy," *Walden,* 1854 (chs. 1 ["As if you could . . . ," p. 33 and "In the long
run . . . ," p. 48], 9 ["Age is no better . . . ," p. 209], and 10, p. 210).
Journal, 1841 (ch. 4), November 11, 1850 (ch. 1, "Some circumstantial . . . ," p. 5),
August 19, 1851 (ch. 11, "How vain it is . . . ," p. 261), 1853 (ch. 12, p. 271);
letter to Daniel Ricketson, August 18, 1857 (ch. 11, "As for style . . . ," p. 259).
James Thurber: *Time,* August 15, 1960 (ch. 7, p. 163).
Alexi Konstantinovich Tolstoy: *Collected Works of Kosma Prutkov,* 1884 (ch. 1, p. 46).
Leo Tolstoy: *Anna Karenina,* 1874, opening words (ch. 9, p. 206).
Lionel Trilling: *The Liberal Imagination,* 1950 (ch. 5, p. 132).
Anthony Trollope: *The Last Chronicle of Barset,* 1866–1867, ch. 17 (ch. 4, p. 109).
Leon Trotsky: *Diary in Exile,* 1935 (ch. 9, p. 207).
Martin Farquhar Tupper:
   "Of Discretion," *Proverbial Philosophy,* 1838–1842 (ch. 11, p. 258).
   "Of Truth in Things False," *Proverbial Philosophy,* 1838–1842 (ch. 1, p. 51).
Mark Twain:
   "The Art Of Composition," *Life as I Find It,* 1890 (ch. 11, "The difference between . . . ,"
   p. 245).
   Autobiography, 1924, vol. 1 (ch. 1, "Biographies are but . . . ," p. 13).
   Notebooks, 1898, ch. 31 (ch. 6, "The radical invents . . . ," p. 157).
   Notebooks, later nineteenth century (chs. 1 ["When people do not . . . ," p. 13] and 4
   ["You must not pay . . . ," p. 115]).
   Pudd'nhead Wilson, 1894 (ch. 10, "Courage is resistance . . . ," p. 214), ch. 19 (ch. 6,
   "It were not best . . . ," p. 145), ch. 66 (ch. 1, "Everyone is a moon . . . ," p. 40).
   "Pudd'nhead Wilson's Calendar" (chs. 1 ["If you pick up . . . ," p. 54], 10 ["Except a
   person . . . ," p. 227], and 11 ["As to the adjective . . . ," p. 252]).
   "Pudd'nhead Wilson's New Calendar," *Following the Equator,* 1897 (chs. 4 ["It takes
   your enemy . . . ," p. 114], 9, p. 196 and 11 ["'Classic' . . . ,"] p. 259).
Frank Tyger: "Scandal Sheet," *Rotary,* Graham, Texas, (ch. 10, p. 224).
Miguel de Unamuno:
   Essays and Soliloquies, 1925 (ch. 2, p. 72).
   Mist, 1914 (ch. 1, "Use harms and . . . ," p. 43).
   The Agony of Christianity, 1928 (ch. 8, "Faith which does . . . ," p. 186).
   The Tragic Sense of Life, 1913, ch. 9 (chs. 1 ["To fall into habit . . . ," p. 51] and 8
   ["Martyrs create . . . ,"] p. 188).
Paul Valéry:
   Quoted in W. H. Auden, *A Certain World,* 1970 (ch. 11, p. 258).
   Mauvaises pensées et autres, 1942 (chs. 6 ["A man who is . . . ," p. 140] and 8, p. 183).
   Tel quel, 1943 (chs. 1 ["If disorder . . . ," p. 53], 3 ["That which has . . . ," p. 89], and
   7, p. 172).

Luc de Clapiers de Vauvenargues: *Réflexions et maximes,* c. 1747 (chs. 1 ["The wicked are . . . ," p. 3 and "When we feel . . . ," p. 57], 2 ["Great success . . . ," p. 67 "The common excuse . . . ," p. 68 "Men despise . . . ," p. 75 and "We are dismayed . . . ," p. 76], 3 ["We discover . . . ," p. 80 "All men are born . . . ," p. 91 and "When you are unwilling . . . ," p. 93], 5, 6 ["The things we know . . . ," p. 149 and "No one is more . . . ," p. 155], and 10, p. 217).

Gore Vidal:
   Quoted in G. Irvine, *Antipanegyric fortom Driberg,* 1976 (ch. 2, "It is not enough . . . ," p. 67).
   New York Times Magazine, September 16, 1973 (ch. 2, "Whenever a friend . . . ," p. 68).

Leonardo da Vinci: *Note Books,* 1508–1518 (chs. 1 ["It is easier . . . ," p. 15 "Vows begin . . . ," p. 15 and "Experience does . . . ," p. 35]).

Virgil:
   Aeneid, 514 B.C.E., book 10, l. 284 (ch. 10, "Fortune favors . . . ," p. 224).
   Minor Poems, Copa, l. 38 (chs. 1, p. 41 and 9, "Death twitches . . . ," p. 207; also quoted by Oliver Wendell Holmes, Jr., on his ninetieth birthday—closing words of a radio address, March 8, 1931).

Voltaire:
   "Le chaponet la poularde," *Dialogues,* 1763 (ch. 4, "Men use thought . . . ," p. 111).
   letter, 1769 (ch. 10); *Sept discours en vers sur l'homme,* 1738 (ch. 4, "The secret of . . . ," p. 104).

Diane von Furstenberg: Reader's Digest, *Quotable Quotes,* 1997 (ch. 9, p. 199).

Marilyn vos Savant: Reader's Digest, *Quotable Quotes,* 1997 (ch. 13, p. 286).

Booker Taliaferro Washington: *Up from Slavery,* 1901 (ch. 10, p. 223).

Daniel Webster: "Argument on the Murder of Captain White," April 6, 1830 (chs. 4, p. 103; 9, p. 204).

Simone Weil: *Gravity and Grace,* 1949 (ch. 1, p. 21).

A. H. Weiler: Privately circulated memorandum, offices of *New York Times* (ch. 1, p. 28).

Arthur Wellesley, Duke of Wellington: Dispatch from the field of Waterloo, June 1815 (ch. 10, p. 220).

Herbert George Wells: *Kipps,* 1905, book 2, ch. 5 (ch. 1, p. 24).

John Wesley: Letter to Joseph Benson, October 5, 1770 (ch. 10, p. 222).

Dame Rebecca West: "The Harsh Voice," *There Is No Conversation,* 1935, sect. 1 (ch. 4, p. 101).

Arthur Waley: "Resignation" by Po Chü-i, translated from Chinese (ch. 6, p. 139).

Dillon Wentworth, Earl of Rosscommon: *Essay on Translated Verse,* 1684, l. 96 (ch. 1, p. 64).

Edith Wharton: "Vesalius in Zante (1564)," *North American Review, 175,* November 1902, pp. 625–31 (ch. 1, p. 34).

Archbishop Richard Whately: *Apophthegms,* 1864 (ch. 5, p. 128).

James McNeill Whistler: *Whistler Versus Ruskin,* 1878 (ch. 1, p. 52).

Alfred North Whitehead: *Adventures of Ideas,* 1932, pt. 4, ch. 19 (ch. 9, p. 201); *Dialogues of Alfred North Whitehead,* 1954 (ch. 11, p. 244).

Walt Whitman: "Preface to the First Edition," *Leaves of Grass,* 1855 (ch. 11, p. 250).

George John Whyte-Melville: *Riding Recollections,* 1878 (ch. 1, p. 31).

Oscar Wilde:

L'Envoi to Rose-leaf and Apple-leaf, 1882 (ch. 1, "One's real life . . . ," p. 8).

A Woman of No Importance, 1893 (chs. 1 ["Everyone is born . . . ," p. 52], 4 ["One should never . . . ," p. 112], 7 ["Nothing spoils . . . ," p. 178], 7 and 9 ["Children begin . . . ," p. 166, p. 202], 8 ["The only difference . . . ," p. 182], and 12, p. 270).

An Ideal Husband, 1893, act 1 (ch. 8, "When the gods . . . ," p. 183).

Aphorisms, 1914, no. 35 (ch. 1, "Simple pleasures . . . ," p. 1, p. 45).

De Profundis, 1905 (ch. 1, "Most people are . . . ," p. 5).

quoted in André Gide, *In Memorium, Oscar Wilde,* 1910 (ch. 11, "I've put my genius . . . ," p. 257).

Lady Windemere's Fan, 1896 (chs. 1 ["Experience is . . . ," p. 14] and 10 ["In this world . . . ," p. 217]).

Oscar Wilde: His Life and Wit, 1946 (ch. 4, "It is always . . . ," p. 111).

Oscariana: The Works of Oscar Wilde—Epigrams, 1909 (ch. 4, "The value of . . . ," p. 114).

The Critic as Artist, 1891 (chs. 6 ["The man who sees . . . ," p. 145 "Nothing that is worth . . . ," p. 144 and "Man is a reasonable . . . ," p. 137] and 11 ["Bad artists . . . ," p. 265).

The Importance of Being Ernest, 1895 (ch. 9, "All women become . . . ," p. 200).

The Picture of Dorian Gray, 1891 (chs. 1 ["One can always be . . . ," p. 6, "There are many things . . . ," p. 18 "A man cannot . . . ," p. 20 "There is luxury . . . ," p. 22 and "I like men who . . . ," p. 57], 7 ["The one charm . . . ," p. 177 and "Those who are faithful . . . ," p. 176], 9 ["The tragedy of old age . . . ," p. 200 and "Conscience and cowardice . . . ," p. 191], 10 ["The only difference . . . ," p. 218 and "The only way to . . . ," p. 215], 11 ["There is no such thing . . . ," p. 257 and "The difference between . . . ," p. 254]).

The Wit and Humor of Oscar Wilde, 1959, (ch. 5, "Consistency is . . . ," p. 120).

Kenneth Williams: "Preface" to *Acid Drops,* 1980 (ch. 11, 253).

John Wilmot, Earl of Rochester: *A Satire Against Mankind,* 1675, l. 20 (ch. 11, p. 236).

Baron Harold Wilson: *Observer,* January 11, 1970 (ch. 11, p. 264).

Oprah Winfrey: Quoted in Nellie Bly, *Oprah!*, 1993; same words stated by Elmer G.
   Leterman in *Reader's Digest*, February 1958 (ch. 9, p. 197).
Jonathan Winters: Reader's Digest, *Quotable Quotes*, 1997 (ch. 11, "If your ship . . . ,"
   p. 246 and "I couldn't wait . . . ," p. 255).
Ludwig Wittgenstein: *Tractatus Logico-Philosophicus*, 1922, p. 148 (ch. 11, p. 249).
Sir Pelham Grenville Wodehouse: "The Man Upstairs," *The Man Upstairs*, 1914 (ch. 1,
   p. 64).
David T. Wolf: As said to Robert Byrne (ch. 6, ,p. 140).
Virginia Woolf: *Writer's Diary*, 1954, entry for August 13, 1921 (ch. 2, p. 69).
Sir Henry Wotton: *A Woman's Heart*, 1651 (ch. 7, p. 166).
William Wrigley Jr.: *Reader's Digest*, July 1940 (ch. 11, p. 233).
Francis Yeats-Brown: *Reader's Digest*, February 1940 (ch. 11, p. 257).
Edward Young:
   Love of Fame, 1725–1728, satire 1, l. 89 (ch. 11, "Some for renown . . . ," p. 238).
   Night Thoughts, 1742–1745, Night 1, l. 390 (ch. 11, "Be wise today . . . ," p. 264),
      l. 393 (ch. 5, "Procrastination is . . . ," p. 128), Night 4, l. 233 (ch. 8, "A God all
      mercy . . . ," p. 182), Night 5, l. 177 (ch. 8, "By night . . . ," p. 185), l. 661 (ch. 1,
      "Like our shadows . . . ," p. 32).